PRAISE FOR *THE LOTUS WITHIN*

"In *The LOTUS Within*, Dr. Amelia Duran-Stanton creatively weaves her life experiences into a tried-and-true process for personal growth. Using tools such as self-introspection, *Ikigai* exploration, purpose-driven discovery, and goal-setting, this book gives the reader a practical template to follow—ultimately shedding light on how to unlock the power and potential within oneself. It's a must-read for those who want to flourish in their personal and professional lives."

—**MARIA MCCONVILLE**, MS, RDN, Army veteran, MilSpouse, MilMom, registered dietitian, entrepreneur

"*The LOTUS Within: Uncovering Your Purpose and Passion in Life* is a gift to each reader for the way it combines and organizes concepts of personal and professional success in workable-sized lessons. There is a sustaining thread of encouragement that serves to inspire continued efforts toward increased efficiency in all facets of life. This book is a masterpiece for its attention to detail and its ability to create the architecture of the 'big picture' of life. I highly recommend *The LOTUS Within*."

—**KATHLEEN E. YANCOSEK**, PhD, author of *Recover in Color*, *Grace & Mercy*, and *Handwriting for Heroes*

"*The LOTUS Within* is a gift to women who want more out of life but find themselves in a catch-22, lacking the bandwidth to read multiple books on the topic. Dr. Duran-Stanton has synthesized best and promising practices and laid them out with a combination of insightful personal stories and practical and achievable activities."

—**DIANE BRUESSOW**, MPAS, PA-C, director of justice, equity, diversity, and inclusion, PA online program, assistant professor, Department of General Internal Medicine, Yale School of Medicine

"Dr. Amelia Duran-Stanton offers the true jugglers of society—women who somehow make things happen despite holding many balls in the air at once—a timeless wisdom and guidance for bringing greater clarity, grace, and purpose to their lives. *The LOTUS Within* offers truly life-affirming advice and excellent strategies for implementing on the ground. In my opinion, the principles apply just as well to men! Highly recommended."

—**DR. MICHAEL SHANDLER**, speaker, life coach, and award-winning author of *Karma and Kismet: A Spiritual Quest Across Continents, Cultures, and Consciousness*

"As a mentor to many professional women, I've often struggled finding resources to help me understand and address their unique challenges. *The LOTUS Within* fills this gap brilliantly. It offers practical strategies for time management, prioritization, and strategic planning that I can confidently recommend to the ambitious women I work with."

—**JOE SIPHER**, founder, product & marketing executive, and author of *Outsmart the Learning Curve: How Ordinary People Can Achieve Extraordinary Success*

"*The LOTUS Within* by Dr. Amelia Duran-Stanton is a transformative guide that empowers women to take charge of their lives through strategic planning and effective time management. I love the concept of blending self-care with practical tools, for anyone seeking to prioritize their goals. As someone who juggles a million things in a fast-paced environment, this book is not just a manual; it's a roadmap for personal and professional growth. Amelia's insights inspire readers to cultivate their inner strength and embrace their potential fully. A must-read!"

—**SAIBATU MANSARAY**, MPAS, MIS, PA-C, founder and CEO of The Mansaray Foundation

"*The LOTUS Within* will be perfect for many of my female patients, including young women in crisis, those experiencing a divorce or contemplating substantial career changes, and seniors drifting in the aftermath of retirement. This book could be particularly useful for any of them (and the men in their lives). I also recommend it for those studying psychiatry and/or psychology."

—**ANANDHI NARASIMHAN**, MD, Cedars Sinai Medical Center, Aviva Family and Children's Services, author of *How Concerned Should I Be? Questions Pertaining to the Developing Mind*

"*The LOTUS Within* is written from the unique vantage point of a seasoned military veteran whose firsthand experience makes her an excellent mentor for women seeking to find their purpose and vision in life, whether they are serving their country or simply trying to take good care of themselves and their family. I wish I had her helping me too!"

—**KATHRYN SMERLING**, PhD, family therapist, New York City, coauthor of *Playtime to Primetime: A Back-to-Basics Toolkit for Healthy Relationships*

"A powerful process of self-inquiry. *The LOTUS Within* process allows the reader to dive deep into their purpose and develop the strategic plan to get there."

—**ADHANA MCCARTHY**, integrative physician assistant, contributing author of *The Future of Sacred Yoga Therapy*

"Amelia brilliantly captures key concepts that have proven to develop the necessary skills to achieve a fulfilling and balanced life. Her practical tools are easy to understand and apply. The step-by-step guide makes readers feel immediately energized to tackle tough questions and engage in introspection. A must-read for all who want to feel empowered to maximize their potential!"

—**DONNA M. CLOUSE**, program director, San Antonio, TX

"Life moves fast. *The LOTUS Within* slowed me down long enough to bring attention to my life and intention to my choices before life got away from me. I'm grateful and better off as a result."

—**CATHY CARROLL**, president of Legacy Onward, Inc, and author of *Hug of War: How to Lead a Family Business with both Love and Logic*

"Using clear definitions and probing questions, Amelia Duran-Stanton's *The LOTUS Within* helps readers evaluate their present state, clarify values, align them with goals, and achieve success as they define it. This is a practical, accessible guide to personal improvement, complete with exercises and examples for implementing the author's ideas."

—**B. LYNN GOODWIN**, author of *Disrupted, Talent,* and *Never Too Late: From Wannabe to Wife at 62*

"*The LOTUS Within* is a lifesaver for busy professional women! Amelia's step-by-step LOTUS system tackles time management struggles head-on. The book is insightful, sharing her unique perspective on overcoming challenges. It's also incredibly practical and includes real-life stories and Q&A sections that make it even more engaging. *LOTUS* provides the tools you need to cultivate your inner fire and the burning passion that fuels your purpose. By uncovering your *why*, you'll thrive and become a radiant source of inspiration for others. Amelia equips you to blossom exactly where you are, ready to share your unique light with the world."

—**MARLENE ARIAS REYNOSO**, nurse and health-care executive leader

"Amelia's book offers valuable lessons on overcoming challenges and developing strong leadership qualities. The real-life examples and practical advice will inspire and equip readers with the tools they need to navigate their own journeys with confidence and resilience."

—**MIRIAM DOUGLAS**, BSN, MM, MHA, doctoral student

"The book is amazing. As soon as I began reading it, I could not put it down. I felt like it was speaking to me, clarifying all the feelings I had as a career woman, mom, and wife, my stress trying to make it all work while feeling that by doing so I am failing at something. Dr. Amelia Duran-Stanton's book puts things in perspective and helps me look deep into myself and start working on 'me' because you cannot pour from an empty glass. The book will remind others that they are not alone and inspire them to work on things that will help them be successful."

—**FIORELLA CECILIA ESAFE**, talent manager for the federal government

"Dr. Amelia Duran-Stanton has been my longtime mentor, both at a distance and in person. Her book *The LOTUS Within* is a simple yet powerful read. It is instrumental in my journey to redefine my routine and define my purpose in life. As we evolve, it is important to reassess to ensure you are calibrated on your journey. This book is a great guide for completing the ongoing reassessment task. The journey to purpose is a daily practice that can easily become deterred secondary to the fast-paced modern life or mundaneness linked with unhappiness. I hadn't deep-dove into the constructs of legacy and orchestrating the narration of my obituary prior to this literature. I think this book can be igniting in any woman's life who is willing to digest and implement the information presented in this book."

—**ARRISA HANSON**, physician assistant/associate

"Dr. Amelia Duran-Stanton is first and foremost my friend, and I will be forever proud to say that. We served together for many years in challenging circumstances, and her work ethic, compassion, and dedication are unrivaled. Best of all, she is positive and unwavering in her commitment to help others. *The LOTUS Within* will help so many people, and I look forward to doing whatever I can to assist her in amplifying her valuable work."

—**ANGELA WILLIAMS**, program manager, Ansbach, Germany

"*The LOTUS Within* provides readers with a safe place to reflect with total honesty. The vignettes shared by other women allow us to see ourselves––our inspirations and motivations, but also our shortcomings, faults, and fears—while providing actionable tools to find our *ikigai*, our *why*, to live a fulfilling life. Amelia's book is a resource I will visit often to assess and reassess how my goals are aligned with my purpose. It will help you create a symbiotic relationship between what you do daily and how that impacts your future self."

—**LINDSEY UMLAUF**, DPT, MBA, MHA, FACHE,
physical therapist and health-care executive leader

"Dr. Amelia Duran-Stanton's book, *The LOTUS Within*, is a powerful testament to the spirit of Bayanihan, embodying solidarity and cooperation among Filipinos worldwide. As a reader inspired by her journey and encouraged by the Filipino community in Germany, I found her approach to self-help refreshing and deeply impactful. *The LOTUS Within* isn't just another generic guide; it's a tailored tool that focuses on effective time management and self-assessment, offering profound insights into personal growth and empowerment, especially for women seeking to regain control of their lives. Amelia's book fills a critical gap in the self-help genre by providing practical, in-depth questions that pinpoint areas for improvement and encourage transformative self-reflection. If you're ready to navigate life's challenges with renewed passion and confidence, this book is an essential companion on your journey to reclaiming your future."

—**MELISSA LEWIS**, physician assistant/associate

"Dr. Amelia Duran-Stanton's book is a powerful guide that intertwines organization and time management with personal fulfillment. It encourages readers to delve into their motivations and values, helping them set clear goals and priorities. Practical strategies for decluttering physical and mental spaces and techniques like time blocking equip readers to enhance productivity and reduce stress. The book's insights into overcoming procrastination and maintaining life balance are particularly valuable in today's fast-paced world. Overall, Amelia has crafted a compelling resource that empowers individuals to lead intentional and productive lives, making it a must-read for anyone seeking clarity and efficiency in their personal and professional pursuits."

—**NATASHA BEBO**, registered nurse and military spouse

"Dr. Amelia Duran-Stanton's book is not only useful for women but also men, for themselves and to help their spouses. It is a blueprint for intentional living, emphasizing the importance of understanding personal motivations to achieve meaningful goals through effective prioritization, organization, and time management. It's a practical guide that resonates deeply with anyone seeking clarity and productivity in their daily lives. By offering strategies to streamline tasks and combat distractions, the book equips readers with tools to navigate challenges and stay focused on what matters most. Overall, Amelia has crafted a valuable resource that not only empowers individuals to enhance their personal efficiency but also fosters a deeper understanding of self and purpose."

—**DANIEL BEBO**, medical specialist

"Amelia's book, *The LOTUS Within*, is a must-read manual that empowers women to unlock their full potential through effective time management, planning, and prioritization techniques essential for career and personal success. It serves as a beacon of empowerment, guiding readers on a journey of personal development and transformation. By fostering clarity and confidence, it enables women to harness their innate abilities and navigate life's challenges with resilience and determination."

—**JENIFER QUIAPO COX**, RN, BSN, primary care nurse and military spouse

"As a fellow physician assistant, I have seen Dr. Duran-Stanton in action. Her work ethic is impeccable, and her generosity of spirit is inspiring to all of us who know her. *The LOTUS Within* will be a goldmine for so many service members and civilians."

—**DAWN ORTA**, human resources leader, aviation physician assistant

"*The LOTUS Within* is a game changer for professional women seeking to reclaim their time and align their lives with purpose. Through its transformative concepts, this book guides you on a journey of self-discovery and reflection, helping you find your ikigai and align your actions with your long-term goals. With practical strategies for strategic planning, prioritization, and time management, *The LOTUS Within* offers a clear path to unlocking your true potential and living a balanced, fulfilling life. A must-read for anyone ready to take control of their future. As an executive coach, I use these same concepts with leaders. *The LOTUS Within* is like an on-call and self-paced executive coach at your fingertips!"

—**SETH VARAYON**, executive coach

"As a fellow physician assistant and military service member, I completely resonated with Dr. Duran-Stanton's lessons throughout *The LOTUS Within*. This gem is filled with applicable introspective tools and practices to help women understand what is important to them and why. It's an essential read for understanding our purpose and reminding ourselves that the world needs our light to shine. Amelia provides a holistic and compassionate path to discovering our purpose and gives us permission, motivation, and encouragement to fulfill it."

—**THERESA KULIKOWSKI-GILLESPIE,** holistic physician assistant, mindfulness meditation teacher, military spouse, and US Army veteran

The LOTUS Within: Grow Your Purpose and Ignite Your Passion

by Amelia Duran-Stanton, PhD, DSc, PA-C

© Copyright 2024 Amelia Duran-Stanton, PhD, DSc, PA-C

ISBN 979-8-88824-551-4

All rights reserved. No part of this publication may be reproduced, stored in a retrieval system, or transmitted in any form or by any means—electronic, mechanical, photocopy, recording, or any other—except for brief quotations in printed reviews, without the prior written permission of the author.

DISCLAIMER: The author's views are theirs and do not reflect the official policy of the United States Army, Department of Defense or the US government.

Published by

köehlerbooks™

3705 Shore Drive
Virginia Beach, VA 23455
800-435-4811
www.koehlerbooks.com

THE LOTUS WITHIN

Amelia Duran-Stanton,
PhD, DSc, PA-C

VIRGINIA BEACH
CAPE CHARLES

DEDICATION

This book is dedicated to my *Apu* Celang, *Lola* Eden, *Lola* Ines, and my mother Luz. My sister, my daughter, my niece, and I stand on the shoulders of strong Filipinas; their lineage continues, and I thank them for the legacy they left behind for us. I continue to pay it forward for all future generations to come.

Dr. Amelia M. Duran-Stanton

TABLE OF CONTENTS

Introduction: Welcome to the Land of LOTUS 1
A Personal Assessment 11

Part One: *What Is Your "Why"?* 13

    Chapter 1: *Mistakes and Secrets* 17

    Chapter 2: *The Importance of Self-Care in Strategic Life Planning* 21

    Chapter 3: *Finding Your Ikigai* 25

    Chapter 4: *Writing Your Obituary* 29

    Chapter 5: *Discovering Your "Why"* 33

    Part One: *Fundamentals Review and Workbook Preview* 41

Part Two: *What Is Your Strategy for the Future?* 43

    Chapter 6: *The Arc of Improvement* 48

    Chapter 7: *Evaluate Your Current State of Self* 55

    Chapter 8: *Reverse Engineer Your Plan* 58

    Part Two: *Fundamentals Review and Workbook Preview* 62

Part Three: *How Do You Prioritize?* 65

    Chapter 9: *Why? How? What?* 68

    Chapter 10: *Conducting a SWOT Analysis* 73

    Chapter 11: *The 7 Habits of Highly Effective People* 75

    Chapter 12: *Prioritization Tools* 81

    Part Three: *Fundamentals Review and Workbook Preview* 83

Part Four: *Can You Manage Your Time?* 85
    Chapter 13: *How to Write SMART Goals* 91
    Chapter 14: *Tools to Help You Manage Time* 96
    Chapter 15: *Wellness and the Zone of Genius* 106
    Part Four: *Fundamentals Review and Workbook Preview* 110

Conclusion: *Reflections of my Own Life Experiences* 111
Part Five: *The Workbook* 115

Acknowledgments: Standing on the Shoulders of Giants 147
References 149

Do Something Today That Your Future Self Will Thank You For!

LOTUS

A

Life of **T**imeless **U**nbound **S**trategies

"Like a lotus flower, we have the ability to rise from mud, grow in darkness, bloom where we are planted, and radiate for others."

—Dr. Amelia M. Duran-Stanton

Artwork by Sofia Duran-Stanton

INTRODUCTION

Welcome to the Land of LOTUS

Life is hard. Like it or not, it's still a man's world, and we women need a helping hand to discover the power within us to unlock our full potential. That's what *The LOTUS Within* is all about. Based on a successful course I designed *with* and *for* military women of all ages and backgrounds, it is now available to everyone.

LOTUS—**L**ife **o**f **T**imeless **U**nbound **S**trategies—is designed for busy professional women like you, in the office, at home, and in your community. Its transformative concepts will take you on a journey of self-discovery and reflection, guiding you to align your actions with your goals. My passion is to help people find *their* passion to be their best selves.

As the subtitle of this book challenges each of us to do, *grow your purpose and ignite your passion.*

I am Amelia Duran-Stanton, born in the Philippines, raised by a single mom, and married with two children. I am Lean Six Sigma master black belt certified and an active member of the US Army for thirty-two years, including eight years enlisted, deployments to Kosovo, Iraq, and Afghanistan, and twenty-four years as a physician assistant/associate. I currently serve as the Army medical specialist Corps specific branch proponent officer at the Medical Center of Excellence in JBSA-Fort Sam Houston, Texas.

I have a PhD in postsecondary and adult education and a doctor of science in PA studies in orthopedics. I have held positions as the officer in charge of the Fort Bragg/Liberty Medical Simulation

Training Center, Interservice Physician Assistant Program (IPAP) clinical coordinator, and inspector general. I was previously deputy chief of the Thermal and Mountain Medicine Division at the United States (US) Army Research Institute of Environmental Medicine (USARIEM) in Natick, Massachusetts, chief of the Ready and Resilient Integration Branch and deputy command surgeon for the Installation Management Command at JBSA-Fort Sam Houston, Texas, and the US Army Health Clinic Ansbach commander, in Bavaria, Germany, prior to my current position.

My awards include the Meritorious Service Medal (six), Army Commendation Award (six), Global War on Terrorism Service Medal, Global War on Terrorism Expeditionary Medal, Combat Medical Badge, and Expert Field Medical Badge. I am a member of the Order of Military Medical Merit, an Iron Major recipient, a Distinguished Fellow of the American Academy of Physician Assistants, and the first PA recipient of the Army Medical Specialist Corps New Horizon Research Award.

Most of all, I am a professional cheerleader for people who would like to embark on a journey of self-reflection, self-improvement, and self-care as they strategically plan for a rewarding and fulfilling life.

As Benjamin Franklin once said, "By failing to plan, you are preparing to fail."

No one wants that, and there is no good reason for anyone to follow a random path that will not take them where they wish to go. *The LOTUS Within* addresses this head-on with practical exercises and actionable tools.

Like a lotus flower, each of us has the ability to rise from the mud, grow in darkness, bloom where we are planted, and radiate for others. So, this work I am doing is not merely a legacy I wish to leave behind. It is my mission to raise all of us, beginning with you.

In today's fast-paced world, it's all too easy to become overwhelmed by the demands of work, family, and a plethora of personal and professional responsibilities. It is difficult to balance personal and professional goals. This is especially true for women of all ages, including those serving in the military and civilians in all walks of life.

Throughout this book, you will meet women who share how the LOTUS method is helping them improve their personal and professional lives in a variety of ways. Imagine the seismic shift from feeling overwhelmed at home and at work to embracing the challenges of career and family by learning new ways to set and meet goals, dealing with the consequences of taking risks and making mistakes, and balancing one's mental health. Names have been changed to protect their identity; pseudonyms of real people are coincidental.

Kathy Lauren, twenty-seven years old and single, has used strategic techniques to plan for her future by making constructive changes to her self-care regimen while learning the value of self-love and battling self-doubt:

> I used to beat myself up every time something didn't go right, but since everything happens for a reason, I must learn what's best for *me* and follow my own path. That means not getting discouraged each time something doesn't go exactly as planned. I remind myself that I'll get there at my own pace in my own way, and the LOTUS method has really helped me build confidence in my own ability to navigate these challenges. I feel more and more equipped to design my future, build my career, communicate with my boyfriend, and even plan to have children. Of course, I still get nervous about certain things, but as I achieve my goals, I know I will be better equipped to give back, be a better nurse, and expand my goals for the future.

Michelle Patterson, fifty-three, a retired Army veteran and mother of one, has been struggling without a concrete strategy for transitioning to a new job back in Texas. While she can control the packing and moving, she's been behind the eight ball when it comes to feeling a sense of calm in her life:

> My biggest challenge when it comes to future planning is that on a day-to-day basis, I have been reactive instead of proactive. I always feel behind and stressed. I work hard, but I have no personal life, which is frustrating. Since I didn't plan well for my future, it's been a punch in the gut, and having huge setbacks really sucks. It's made me tired, sad, and depressed. The techniques I am learning through the LOTUS method are now helping me balance having more time with my patients while still managing enough time for the important work of managing notes. I'm making progress so that I can enjoy my work more and become a much happier health-care provider. I'm working less, my patients feel well taken care of, and I enjoy working again! A happy provider means happy patients, and I'm living proof of that, as I continue my path to meeting my goal of helping people in my community, including veterans and those in homeless shelters. I now intend to work out more, enjoy family, and have time for myself.

Nicole Baker is forty-two years old. She lives in Bethesda, Maryland, with her husband and one child, with another one away at college. She is learning the art of strategic soft and hard planning, and while she still feels discombobulated at times, she is gathering LOTUS tools to deal with the challenges of military life:

> When I do not plan well for my future, especially allocating time and strategizing career moves, I end up feeling sad and upset that I have allowed other people to impede on my time management when I should have been working on myself. I am moving toward empowering myself through prayer and networking, and you could say I am a work in progress!

Eventually, I know I can reach an ideal situation where I can do whatever I want so that my husband and I, each in charge of our own business, are free to travel and run the show. That's when I see sunshine and happiness entering our lives.

Maria Delgado, fifty, is a mother of three stepchildren. She is working on her PhD and plans her life three to six months in advance, but she wants to plan for life at age sixty-five-plus:

My family and friends get upset when I'm anal about making plans, especially when I become worried about my plan not being achievable. A lot of people rely on me now, and since they are aging and somewhat overwhelmed, it falls heavily on me, which leads me to feeling like I am ill prepared, not well organized, and neglecting things I shouldn't. This causes anxiety. I see the LOTUS methods as a ticket to improving all these issues, and I look forward to better health across the board––physically, emotionally, and financially––which will decrease my stress and allow me to take better care of myself.

Juana Castillo, forty-three, is working on a three-year master's degree program. She is fortunate to have support from her husband, a minimally stressful job close to home, and good health. However, she is anxious about school, her technology skills, and her future:

My biggest challenge when it comes to future planning is time management and how to balance my priorities when it comes to health and work. I feel like I'm missing things I could be doing because I'm not sufficiently organized, and it causes anxiety when I neglect important things. I'm trying to involve my husband more in decision-making and asking for help too, but this isn't always easy for me to do. I'm dreaming of a life with less stress, which also allows me to achieve my goals: a six-figure income and more money to invest in my own business. I'd like to retire early, stay home, and spend more time with my children.

Amanda Lester, MPAS, PA-C, thirty, and a brand-new mother, is from the Philippines. After joining the Army, she completed the Interservice PA Program (IPAP) and attended my course. She said,

> After living in the US for eight years, I realized how fast-paced life here can be. It's a struggle to juggle different roles—— student, soldier, friend, sister, daughter, and wife——without compromising something because I am overextended with so many responsibilities. I thought I could multitask fairly well, especially if I was consistent, but I've come to realize that my "best" does not always yield the same results, and I can't do everything on my own without spreading myself too thin.

When I consider the situations of these women, I realize that the biggest challenges they face revolve around effective planning for the future. When that's not happening, it affects their health and sense of well-being, which can add to common "preexisting conditions," such as feeling overworked and overwhelmed.

One of my mentees puts it like this:

> I am okay in life, but sometimes I cannot catch up. In my case, it's an ongoing mix of procrastination, unpredictable events, health, family, and self-improvement. Prioritization is my weakness. I know I need to stay fit and healthy, but I love wine and sweets. It's a constant battle to find balance. If I want to be happy, then I can't be perfect! I fluctuate between a size four and six. This means I need to exercise, but I must also dedicate time to doing homework——helping my kids with theirs and doing mine. I guess it comes as no surprise that I sometimes struggle with time management!

Living in a society where women can so easily be made to feel like there is always a need to "perform" can be exhausting and draining. Most of us feel like *I have to do it myself* to control the outcome. This leads to a struggle to find time and energy to devote to all areas of one's life.

Hearing so many women share their struggles with time management led me to develop the LOTUS method. I have gained so much wisdom from observing how they deal with their individual situations—some successfully and some not—and this has led me to help them formulate an approach that cultivates prevention, resilience, and, most of all, empowerment.

The LOTUS Within is a transformative guide for any woman seeking to unleash her true potential in strategic planning, prioritization, and time management––at home, at work, and in her community. It offers a proven, step-by-step approach to navigate these challenges, gain clarity of purpose, and develop effective strategies for success.

The journey for each of us begins with discovering our *ikigai*, the Japanese concept of finding our true passion and purpose in life. Through a series of thought-provoking exercises and prompts, readers uncover their unique strengths, talents, and values that guide their path forward. By aligning our actions with our *ikigai*, we can experience a greater sense of fulfillment and motivation in our personal and professional endeavors.

Reflecting on our past self is a key component of *The LOTUS Within*. By exploring our past experiences, successes, and challenges, we gain valuable insights and lessons that will inform our strategic planning and decision-making. Reflecting on our past self helps us assess our current state and identify patterns, strengths, and areas for improvement. Each step allows us to craft a vision for our future and make more informed choices moving forward.

This is the empowerment I am offering with *The LOTUS Within*. Assessing our past and present behavior and how we operate is critical. You will evaluate how you plan strategically, prioritize tasks (a *big* essential), and manage your time. This assessment will allow you to identify inefficiencies or gaps in your approach and provide a solid foundation for implementing new strategies and habits that work specifically for *you* and *your* needs. This will include an exploration of the concept of identifying your big and little rocks, which helps you focus on your priorities and develop a clear roadmap for achieving your goals. Chapter 8 will delve more in depth into the big and little rocks.

Once we gain clarity of purpose, reflect on our past, and assess our current state, we are ready to craft our vision for the future. I will guide you to define your own meaningful goals that align with your values and aspirations. Then, you can develop an action plan to bridge the gap between your current reality and your desired outcomes.

Artwork by Sofia Duran-Stanton

Last, I will ask you to focus on taking time to care for yourself first before others, including taking a holistic approach to self-care, such as physical, mental, spiritual, and psychological self-care. Remember: self-care is not selfish. It is essential for your overall health and well-being and can be strategic in most aspects of your life.

This process, full of practical exercises and actionable steps, empowers women to make intentional choices, focus on what truly matters, and ultimately become a master of their time, confident in their decisions, and able to prioritize their welfare *without* feeling guilty. This path encourages self-reflection and growth, two pillars of achieving greater success and fulfillment.

Military and civilian spouses experience *loss of self* as a direct result of caring for their partner. This often leads to feeling invisible or overlooked by mental health services, leaving many women to fall short when it comes to managing their partner's care. They need help! Understanding their experiences and difficulties is a central factor in how *The LOTUS Within* has been crafted. The tools it provides will contribute to a better understanding of how their interactions can support or implicate their partner's recovery, and equally important, it offers a way forward for these women to take care of themselves and their families.

I developed *The LOTUS Within* after years of mentoring, coaching, and teaching, which provided me with a deep understanding of the challenges faced by professional women. The content is informed by their stories, along with research, best practices, and real-life examples.

The LOTUS Within goes beyond quick-fix solutions and aims to instill lasting changes. Discovering your purpose and aligning your actions fosters personal and professional growth that extends beyond your initial reading experience. I hope it will become an indispensable companion on your journey to becoming a master planner, prioritizer, and time manager.

As Madonna once said, "A lot of people are afraid to say what they want. That's why they don't get what they want." It's time for *you* to get what *you* want!

The workbook sections will empower you to take control of your time, make confident decisions, and create a life of purpose, productivity, and fulfillment. Let's unlock your full potential and embark on a transformative journey of self-discovery, balance, and success.

A PERSONAL ASSESSMENT

Before you continue, I highly recommend you start writing on a journal and take some time to answer these questions as best as you can. I'm sure that you'll soon discover more about yourself, which will change at least some of your answers. In fact, you'll have a chance to *re*assess yourself at the end of part one.

1. Describe the importance of future planning and how you currently plan for your future.
2. What is your biggest challenge when it comes to planning your future?
3. Describe how you currently prioritize.
4. What is your biggest challenge in prioritizing?
5. Describe how you currently manage your time.
6. What is your biggest challenge in time management?
7. Describe the process of how you make important decisions that affect your future.
8. What is your biggest challenge in decision-making for future outcomes?

PART ONE

WHAT IS YOUR "*WHY*"?

What Is Your "Why"?

In today's fast-paced world, many women are juggling multiple roles that define their professional careers and personal lives. With so much on their plates, it's no surprise that they can become overwhelmed and lose sight of their goals and passions. That's why it's especially crucial for professional women to take the time to strategically plan their lives, find their passion, prioritize, and manage their time effectively.

This could be you or someone you know.

Imagine a thirty-two-year-old, professional woman, well-educated, and married with two children. Maybe she's forty-two and overwhelmed at work and home. She is motivated and typically puts other people's needs ahead of her own. She takes life one day at a time. She would like to strategically plan for her future and be more organized, but she cannot seem to carve out the time to do it. She is having difficulty prioritizing herself and her time while juggling her career and taking care of her family. She has moments of self-doubt, and her health is incrementally suffering due to stress and diminishing self-worth.

Sound familiar? Keep reading! This woman can be helped, and so can you.

First and foremost, strategic life planning will allow you to identify your passions and align your personal and professional goals accordingly. When you are clear about what you want to achieve, and why, you are more likely to remain focused and motivated, even in the face of adversity, and we all know that this little devil lurks around almost every corner.

By prioritizing your tasks and responsibilities, you can ensure that you are making the most of your time and energy. This means taking a step back and assessing what tasks are most important and what can be delegated or even eliminated altogether. By prioritizing your time and effort, you can reduce stress and increase your overall sense of satisfaction and fulfillment.

Effective time management is also critical. By creating a schedule and sticking to it, you can maximize your productivity while still leaving time for self-care and important activities. This means saying "No" to unnecessary obligations and delegating tasks to others when possible.

Strategic life planning is not a one-time event. It's an ongoing process. As your professional priorities and circumstances change, you must continue to reevaluate your goals and adjust your plans accordingly. (The workbook sections will help you do that.)

This process requires dedication, commitment, and a willingness to adjust as needed. With the right mindset and approach, you can successfully navigate your many roles, keep multiple balls in the air, and achieve success in all aspects of your life.

CHAPTER 1

Mistakes and Secrets

When I was younger, I was not responsible for my daily activities. My schedule was based on what was given to me by adults. When and what I ate was dictated. The classes I had to attend were based on a schedule I was given, depending on my grade. When I went to basic training after high school, it wasn't any different. My schedule was based on what was already scheduled. I went about my day-to-day being told what to do, what time to wake up, where to march, when to eat, and when to go to bed.

I'm sure you have been in this predicament—when everything you did was prescribed and you went about your daily activities being told what to do. When I arrived at my first duty station, I already knew that I wanted to do certain things in life. I wanted a strong educational background, and I was determined to make it in the military. However, I was still going through the motions of what I was required to do each day. I had the work ethic and discipline to continue my education in the evenings.

I learned that I had several roles in life: soldier, student, patient administrator, daughter, and sister. I had a list of all my roles and what I needed to do for each one. It kept me grounded and focused. But I really did not have a method to determine what my long-term goals were. I was living based on what I thought I should have been doing because of my roles.

Mistakes

Here are ten common mistakes that professional women make when strategically planning their lives, especially when they do not prioritize themselves or manage their time effectively:

1. Not taking the time to reflect on values and passions before making life decisions.
2. Failing to prioritize self-care and neglecting physical, mental, and emotional health.
3. Overcommitting and taking on too many responsibilities.
4. Not setting clear goals and objectives for personal and professional purposes.
5. Being too rigid in their plans and failing to adapt to changing circumstances.
6. Not delegating tasks effectively or failing to ask for help when needed.
7. Failing to recognize the importance of downtime and relaxation in preventing burnout.
8. Getting caught up in minor tasks and losing sight of the bigger picture.
9. Procrastinating or putting off important tasks until the last minute.
10. Being unrealistic about the time and energy needed for tasks and responsibilities.

By recognizing and avoiding these common mistakes, professional women can better plan their lives, prioritize their time, and achieve their goals while still maintaining their overall well-being and sense of fulfillment.

I've met so many women struggling with procrastination,

unexpected events, health issues, family drama, and an ongoing battle to incorporate self-improvement into their lives. Prioritizing is a conundrum for many of them. Far too often, they get sidetracked from their own path because they focus too much on the needs of family, friends, and their community. I get it. It's easy to be the person who helps others. But what about *you*?

Secrets

Here are ten secrets that professional women can use to strategically plan their lives, prioritize themselves, and manage their time effectively:

1. Take time to reflect on values, passions, and long-term goals before making decisions.
2. Prioritize self-care and reduce stress with exercise, healthy food, and meditation or yoga.
3. Use a planner or calendar to schedule time for work and personal responsibilities.
4. Set realistic goals and break them down into smaller, manageable tasks.
5. Learn to say "No" to commitments that do not align with your goals or values.
6. Delegate tasks effectively and ask for help when needed.
7. Make time for downtime and relaxation to prevent burnout and recharge your batteries.
8. Focus on high-value tasks and avoid getting bogged down by low-priority distractions.
9. Set boundaries around your time and learn to prioritize your own needs.
10. Reassess and adjust plans as circumstances change or as you achieve your goals.

By following these secrets, professional women can create a more balanced and fulfilling life while still achieving their personal and professional goals.

Q&A with Maria Delgado

Maria is a fifty-year-old military veteran with over twenty years of active-duty military service. She was a human resource specialist with experience ranging from field units to military medical treatment facilities. She is now pursuing her lifelong goal of earning a doctorate degree, which she began upon completing her military service.

Q: Which mistakes and secrets resonate for you, and why?

A: Overcommitting. I tend to take on too many responsibilities. This leaves me stretched too thin, which compromises my effectiveness. I need to learn to say "No" to commitments that do not align with my goals or values.

Q: What mistakes would you include if you were writing your own chapter 1?

A: Extreme perfectionism.

Q: What secrets would you include, and why?

A: Extreme perfectionism can cause women to set unrealistically high standards for themselves, which can lead to stress and self-doubt. Everything must be done in moderation.

CHAPTER 2

The Importance of Self-Care in Strategic Life Planning

Let's discuss the importance of taking the time to care for yourself first before others and how it can be strategic when you approach time management and prioritization. We'll also explore why self-care is not being selfish and how it can benefit your family.

As Diane Von Furstenberg once said, "The most important relationship in your life is the relationship you have with yourself. Because no matter what happens, you will always be with yourself, so you might as well enjoy the company."

Holistic Health

When it comes to self-care, it is essential to take a holistic approach. This means taking care of your physical, mental, spiritual, and psychological well-being. Neglecting any of these areas can have a significant impact on your overall health and well-being.

Physical Self-Care

This involves taking care of your body, including exercise, healthy eating, and getting enough sleep. Taking care of your physical health can help you feel energized and motivated, allowing you to tackle your goals with more focus and clarity.

Mental Self-Care

Taking care of your mind is critical to your health and happiness. It includes practicing mindfulness, engaging in activities you enjoy, and seeking support when needed.

Taking care of your mental health can help you reduce stress and anxiety, allowing you to approach your goals with a clear and positive mindset.

Spiritual Self-Care

Nurturing your spirit or soul is as important as taking care of your body. This includes engaging in activities that bring you peace and fulfillment, such as meditation, prayer, or spending time in nature. Taking care of your spiritual health can help you find meaning and purpose in life, which can be an essential motivator in achieving your goals.

Psychological Self-Care

This involves taking care of your emotional well-being, including practicing self-compassion, setting boundaries, and seeking professional help when needed. Taking care of your psychological health can help you develop resilience and cope with life's challenges, allowing you to stay focused on your goals.

Self-Care Is Not Selfish

Many people believe that taking care of themselves first is selfish, but the truth is that self-care is essential to being able to care for others effectively. When you neglect your own needs, you may become overwhelmed, stressed, and unable to provide the support and care that your family and loved ones need. Taking care of yourself is not only beneficial for you but also for those around you. When you prioritize self-care, you are better equipped to manage your time effectively, prioritize your goals, and support your family and loved ones.

Strategic Self-Care

Self-care can also be strategic in planning your life, managing time, and prioritizing. By taking care of yourself, you can develop the energy, focus, and clarity needed to tackle your goals effectively. For example, if you prioritize exercise as part of your physical self-care routine, you may find that you have more energy and focus throughout the day, allowing you to be more productive and efficient with your time. Self-care can also help you develop the resilience and coping skills needed to manage stress and challenges effectively, allowing you to stay focused on your goals and priorities.

It Is About You!

Self-care is not selfish. It's essential for your overall health and well-being. By taking a holistic approach to self-care, including physical, mental, spiritual, and psychological well-being, you can develop the energy, focus, and clarity needed to tackle your goals effectively.

Self-care can also be strategic in planning your life, managing time, and prioritizing. So, take the time to care for yourself first, and you'll be better equipped to care for your family and loved ones effectively. Remember, self-care is not a luxury but rather a necessity for a fulfilling and balanced life.

Juana Craven, RN, a busy mom with a demanding job who is also going to school full-time, demonstrates why people who struggle with life planning, time management, and prioritization ultimately sacrifice their own self-care and fall short of achieving success.

"I am the one who helps people when they need it," says Juana. "I always offer support. A lot of people think I am too nice, but I dedicate my time to these people because that's just how I am. This means I often encounter unexpected situations with my parents and relatives when someone needs my help. For example, my mom will send me some documents that she does not understand, such as laboratory results, bank statements, or letters from an insurance company. I have to help her. I also drive her to frequent medical appointments because she does not drive on the highway or in unfamiliar locations. I take care of everyone, but I love to socialize too, so this is a problem. I love to go out and drink with my friends, but if I do, on top of everything else, I'm exhausted the next day and need a nap, which I don't have time to take! I guess if you consider all these factors in my life, it's no wonder that I sometimes struggle with time management. On top of that, I still can't figure out how to take care of myself."

Juana is not alone in her daily struggles. Just about every woman I have met during my time in the military, including soldiers, spouses, administrative personnel, and civilian support staff, is behind the eight ball when it comes to self-care. I'm right there with these women too, struggling to love myself as much as I love everyone else.

Perhaps Eartha Kitt put it best when she said, "It's all about falling in love with yourself and sharing that love with someone who appreciates you, rather than looking for love to compensate for a self-love deficit."

No matter where you might be on this spectrum of self-love, we *all* can improve our methods for self-care. Remember, when you take care of yourself well, you can take care of others even better.

CHAPTER 3

Finding Your Ikigai

Ikigai is a Japanese concept that roughly translates to "a reason for being." It is a combination of passion, mission, vocation, and profession that gives your life purpose and meaning. According to the Japanese, everyone has an *ikigai*, but it takes time and effort to discover it. In this chapter, we will explore the concept of *ikigai* and how you can find your own.

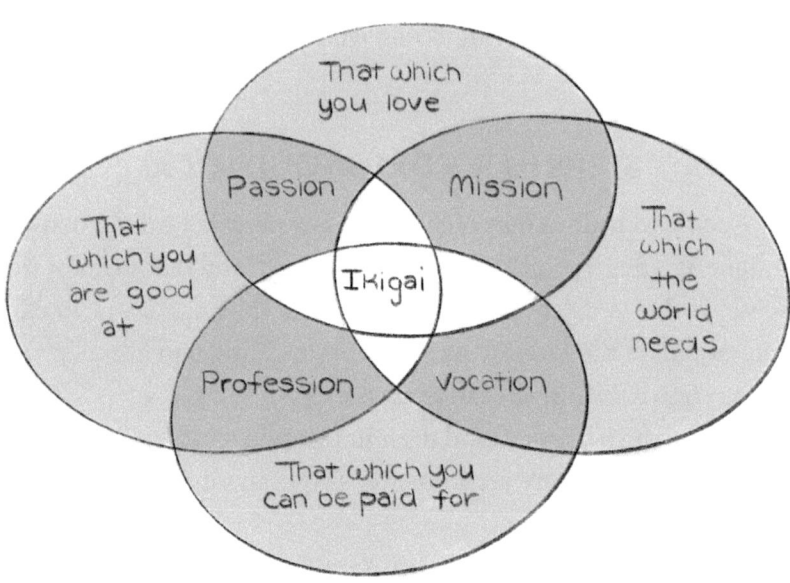

Artwork by Sofia Duran-Stanton

UNDERSTANDING THE CONCEPT OF *IKIGAI*

To find your *ikigai*, you first need to understand what it means. Let's break it down:

Passion. This is what you love doing. It is what gets you excited and motivates you to get out of bed in the morning. Passion is the deep interest and enthusiasm you have for something. It is the thing that makes you feel alive, fulfilled, and motivated. Passion can be found in any aspect of life, such as hobbies, career, relationships, or personal development. Identifying your passion is essential for life planning because it helps you align your values with your goals. When you pursue your passion, you feel more fulfilled and purposeful, and your work and life have more meaning.

Mission. This is your purpose in life. It is the impact you want to make on the world and the legacy you want to leave behind.

Vocation. This is what you're good at. It is your natural talent and the skills you've developed over the years.

Profession. This is what you can get paid for. It is the career that allows you to make a living doing what you love and what you're good at.

STEPS IN FINDING YOUR *IKIGAI*

"I've come to believe that each of us has a personal calling that's as unique as a fingerprint," says Oprah Winfrey, "and that the best way to succeed is to discover what you love and then find a way to offer it to others in the form of service, working hard, and also allowing the energy of the universe to lead you."

Now that you understand the four components of *ikigai*, it's time to find your own. Here are some steps you can take:

Step 1: Identify Your Passions

What activities make you lose track of time? What hobbies do you enjoy? What topics do you love learning about? These are all clues to your passions. Make a list of everything you love doing, no matter how big or small.

Step 2: Determine Your Mission

What do you want to accomplish in life? What kind of impact do you want to make on the world? What do you want to be remembered for? Write down your answers to these questions and see if you can identify a common theme.

Step 3: Recognize Your Talents

What are you naturally good at? What skills have you developed over the years? What do others compliment you on? Make a list of your talents and skills.

Step 4: Find Your Profession

What careers align with your passions, mission, and talents? Research different industries and job roles to see what resonates with you. Talk to people who work in those fields to get a better understanding of what the job entails.

Step 5: Combine Your Passions, Mission, Talents, and Profession

Now that you have identified your passions, mission, talents, and profession, it is time to combine them to find your *ikigai*. Look for areas where they overlap and see if you can find a career that allows you to do what you love, make an impact, use your skills, and get paid for it.

LIVING YOUR *IKIGAI*

Finding your *ikigai* is just the first step. The next is to live it. Here are tips for doing so:

Set goals. Once you have identified your *ikigai*, set goals that align with it. This will help you stay motivated and focused.

Act. Don't just talk about your *ikigai*. Act toward it. Start small and work your way up.

Embrace challenges. Pursuing your *ikigai* is not always easy. Embrace challenges as opportunities for growth and learning.

Surround yourself with supportive people. Find people who believe in your *ikigai* and support you in pursuing it.

Be patient. Finding and living your *ikigai* takes time. Be patient and enjoy the journey.

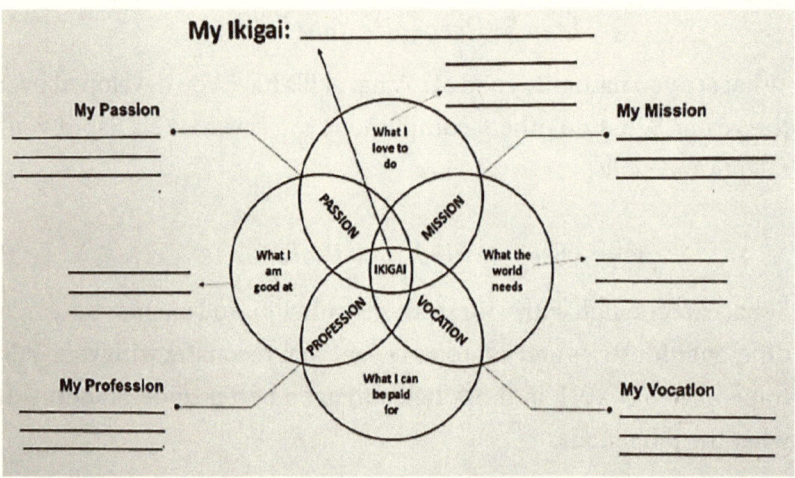

You can use this or create your own visual system for exploring your personal ikigai.

YOUR *IKIGAI* IS FLUID

Finding your *ikigai* is a lifelong journey. It requires self-reflection, exploration, and a willingness to take risks. But the rewards are worth it. When you find your *ikigai*, you will experience a sense of fulfillment, purpose, and joy that cannot be found elsewhere.

Remember, your *ikigai* may change over time as your passions, talents, and mission evolve. That's okay. Embrace the changes and continue to pursue what brings you meaning and happiness.

CHAPTER 4

Writing Your Obituary

Death is a difficult topic to discuss, but it is important to plan for it. One way to plan for your death is by writing your obituary.

Why Write Your Obituary?

Writing your obituary may seem morbid, but it can be an empowering and meaningful process. Here are some reasons why you should consider writing your obituary:

Control Your Legacy

Writing your obituary allows you to control your legacy. You can share your life story and accomplishments in your own words, ensuring that your loved ones and future generations understand your values and achievements.

Reduce the Burden on Your Loved Ones

When you pass away, your loved ones will be grieving and overwhelmed. By writing your obituary ahead of time, you can reduce the additional burden on your family during their grief and ensure that your wishes are followed.

Reflect on Your Life

Writing your obituary now provides an opportunity to reflect on your entire life and the impact you've made. It can help you clarify your values, set goals, and make positive changes in your life.

HOW TO GET STARTED

Writing your obituary doesn't have to be daunting. Here are some steps to get started:

Step 1: Gather information.

Start by gathering information about your life, such as your birth date, education, career, and family. You can also include hobbies, interests, and accomplishments.

Step 2: Decide on the tone.

Think about the tone you want to convey in your obituary. Do you want it to be serious or lighthearted? Reflective or celebratory? This will help guide the content and style of your obituary.

Step 3: Write a draft.

Using the information you've gathered, write a draft of your obituary. Don't worry about making it perfect; you can always revise it later.

Step 4: Revise and edit.

Review your draft and make any necessary revisions or edits. Consider asking a trusted friend or family member to review it as well.

Step 5: Share your wishes.

Once your obituary is complete, share it with your loved ones and discuss your wishes for your funeral or memorial service. Even though you're not my loved one (yet), allow me to share my obituary on the next page, which, of course, is subject to change as my life evolves.

Writing your obituary is a powerful way to reflect on your life and ensure that your legacy is remembered as you wish. By taking control of this process, you can reduce the burden on your loved ones, create a meaningful tribute to your life, and strategically plan your life as you live it now.

Dearly beloved, we are gathered here today to celebrate the life of Amelia Denan-Stanton.

We remember her as a wife, mother, friend and colleague who dedicated much of her life in helping others.

Her passion: to leave this world a better place than she found it. With that said, she has certainly succeeded!

You see here before you are everyone whose life she has touched. She made a great impact. As we celebrate Amelia's life and legacy, her memory lives on for future generations to come.

In her life's work she improved the lives of many in improving outlooks and inspired others to become their best selves.

CHAPTER 5

Discovering Your "Why"

Gretchen Rubin, author of *The Happiness Project*, states that self-knowledge is a key to happiness, and "we can build happy lives only on the foundation of our own nature, our own interests, our own values, our own temperament."

This is the key to unlocking your life's purpose.

When it comes to strategic life planning, identifying your passion, prioritization, and time management, it is easy to get caught up in the "what" and "how" of achieving your goals. However, it is equally important to explore the *why*—the underlying motivation and purpose that drives your actions.

In Japanese culture, this concept is known as *ikigai*, the reason for being. It is the intersection of what you love, what you're good at, what the world needs, and what you can be paid for. When you have a strong sense of *ikigai*, you're able to align your personal values and strengths with your career, relationships, and overall life goals.

But how do you discover your *why* and define your *ikigai*? Here are the steps:

Reflect on your past experiences. Think back to moments in your life when you felt most fulfilled, energized, and purposeful. What were you doing? Who were you with? What values or beliefs did you uphold? These clues give insight into your passions and strengths.

Identify your core values. Values are the guiding principles that shape our beliefs, attitudes, and actions. They are the things that matter most to us, such as honesty, integrity, respect, family, spirituality, and creativity. Consider what principles are most important to you in life, such as family, community, creativity, or service. When you live in alignment with your values, you feel more authentic and fulfilled.

When you identify your values, you have a clearer understanding of who you are, what motivates you, and what you want to achieve in life. Your values act as a compass that guides your decisions and actions and helps you prioritize your time and energy.

Visualize your ideal future. Imagine yourself in ten, twenty, or thirty years. What kind of life do you want to be living? What accomplishments do you want to have achieved? This can help you clarify your long-term goals and aspirations.

Experiment and explore. Don't be afraid to try new things and step out of your comfort zone. Pursue hobbies, volunteer opportunities, or educational programs that align with your interests and values. This can help you gain new skills, build relationships, and refine your sense of purpose.

Once you've discovered your *why* and defined your *ikigai*, you can use it as a guiding star in your strategic life planning. You can prioritize your time and energy for activities that align with your values and purpose and delegate or eliminate tasks that don't. You can make career choices that are in line with your passions and strengths and cultivate relationships that nourish your soul. You can set realistic goals and create action plans that are driven by a deep sense of motivation and purpose.

Discovering your *why* is not just a fluffy, feel-good exercise. It is a crucial step in strategic life planning, prioritization, and time management. When you have a strong sense of purpose and motivation, you're better equipped to navigate life's challenges and opportunities with grace and resilience. So, take the time to explore your *ikigai* and define your *why*. Your life will be all the richer for it.

REFLECTION ON YOUR PAST

As we grow older, it is natural to reflect on where we came from and how we got to where we are today. Our childhood experiences shape who we are and can have a profound impact on our adult lives. In this chapter, we'll explore the importance of reflecting on your childhood and how it can help you understand yourself better.

Artwork by Sofia Duran-Stanton

WHY REFLECTING ON YOUR CHILDHOOD IS IMPORTANT

Our childhood experiences shape our beliefs, values, and behaviors. They influence how we view the world and ourselves. By reflecting on our childhood, we can gain a deeper understanding of why we think and act the way we do. This can help us identify patterns and behaviors that no longer serve us and make positive changes in our lives.

Reflecting on your childhood can also help you with the following.

Develop self-awareness. Understanding your childhood experiences can help you become more self-aware and recognize your strengths and weaknesses.

Improve relationships. Childhood experiences can impact how we relate to others. Reflecting on these experiences can help us improve our relationships with others.

Heal past wounds. Childhood trauma can have lasting effects on our mental health. Reflecting on these experiences can help us identify unresolved issues and work toward healing.

HOW TO REFLECT ON YOUR CHILDHOOD

Reflecting on your childhood can be a challenging and emotional process. Here are some steps you can take to make the process easier:

Step 1: Create a safe space.

Find a quiet and safe space where you can reflect without distractions or interruptions. This can be a room in your home or a quiet outdoor space.

Step 2: Gather memories.

Gather items that remind you of your childhood, such as old photos, toys, or letters. These can help trigger memories and emotions.

Step 3: Journal.

Write down your memories and feelings as they come up. This can help you process your emotions and gain insight into your experiences.

Step 4: Seek support.

Reflecting on your childhood can be difficult. Consider seeking support from a therapist or trusted friend to help you through the process.

WHAT TO LOOK FOR WHEN REFLECTING ON YOUR CHILDHOOD

When reflecting on your childhood, look for patterns and behaviors that have continued into your adult life. Here are some things to consider:

Relationships with caregivers. How did you relate to your parents or caregivers? What kind of relationship did you have with them?

Family dynamics. What was the dynamic between you and your siblings or other family members? How did your family function as a unit?

Traumatic experiences. Did you experience any traumatic events in your childhood, such as abuse or neglect?

Interests and passions. What were your interests and passions as a child? How have they evolved over time?

REFLECT ON HOW YOU ARRIVED WHERE YOU ARE TODAY

Reflecting on how you got to where you are today is a powerful exercise that allows you to gain a better understanding of your journey and the factors that have shaped your life. It can also help you identify patterns, strengths, weaknesses, and opportunities for growth.

To begin this exercise, take some time to think about your life story. Start by recalling your earliest memories and working your way forward to the present day. Consider the different phases of your life, such as childhood, adolescence, early adulthood, and where you are now.

QUESTIONS TO ASK YOURSELF

What were the defining moments or experiences during this time?

Who were the people that influenced me the most?

What were the challenges that I faced?

What were the successes that I achieved?

What were the lessons that I learned?

Take notes as you go through this exercise. Be as specific and detailed as possible. Think about the emotions that you felt during each phase, and identify the values, beliefs, and goals that guided your decisions.

Once you have a clear picture of your life story, you can begin to identify patterns and themes. Perhaps you notice that you have always been drawn to helping others, or you tend to be a risk-taker. Maybe you see that you have a natural talent for a particular skill or activity.

As you identify these patterns and themes, start to consider how they align with your values and passions. Do they support your overall sense of purpose and meaning in life? If not, how can you adjust your priorities and goals to better align with what truly matters to you?

Reflecting on how you got to where you are today can also help you set more effective goals and make better decisions about your future. By understanding your past experiences and what led you to where you are today, you can be more intentional about the choices you make going forward. You can prioritize the things that truly matter to you and ensure that your actions align with your values and purpose.

Overall, reflecting on your life story is a powerful tool for personal growth and development. It can help you gain clarity and perspective on your journey, identify patterns and themes, and make more intentional choices about your future.

REFLECT ON YOUR SIGNIFICANT MILESTONES TO DATE

Exploring your significant milestones so far can be a helpful way to reflect on your past achievements and consider the path that you want to take going forward. Significant milestones can include personal achievements, such as graduation, marriage, or the birth of a child, as well as professional achievements, such as getting a promotion or starting a successful business.

To begin this exercise, start by making a list of significant milestones that you have achieved so far in your life. Consider the different areas of your life, such as career, education, family, personal growth, and relationships. Write down each milestone and take a moment to reflect on what it meant to you at the time.

As you reflect on each milestone, ask yourself the following.

What was the significance of this milestone for me at the time?

What did I learn from achieving this milestone?

How did this milestone impact my life going forward?

Did achieving this milestone align with my values and passions?

Was this milestone part of a larger goal or plan that I had for myself?

Once you have identified your significant milestones, look for patterns and themes. Are there commonalities between the achievements that have been most meaningful to you? Are there any gaps that you would like to fill in your journey so far?

Use this reflection as an opportunity to celebrate your accomplishments and acknowledge the hard work and dedication that has brought you to where you are today. It can also help you gain clarity about what truly matters and how you want to shape your future.

As you consider your significant milestones, think about what you would like to achieve in the future. What goals and aspirations do you have for yourself? How can you use the lessons and experiences of your past achievements to inform your future plans?

Overall, exploring your significant milestones so far can be a valuable exercise in reflection and goal-setting. It can help you gain perspective on your journey, celebrate your accomplishments, and set the stage for a fulfilling and purposeful future.

Reflecting on your childhood can be a challenging but rewarding process. By gaining a deeper understanding of your childhood experiences, you can make positive changes in your life and improve your relationships with others. Remember, it is never too late to heal past wounds and create a better future for yourself.

PART ONE

Fundamentals Review and Workbook Preview

Now that you've completed part one, try the personal assessment again and see how your perspective may have changed.

A PERSONAL ASSESSMENT

1. Describe the importance of future planning and how you currently plan for your future.
2. What is your biggest challenge when it comes to planning your future?
3. Describe how you currently prioritize.
4. What is your biggest challenge in prioritizing?
5. Describe how you currently manage your time.
6. What is your biggest challenge in time management?
7. Describe the process of how you make important decisions that affect your future.
8. What is your biggest challenge in decision-making for future outcomes?

Consider the following list of suggestions to put you on a positive path to finding your own *ikigai* and making it a viable and winning part of your life. (Remember, this test is fluid.)

EXERCISES AND TAKEAWAYS

1. Write your obituary.
2. Explore your *"why"* (passion, values, strengths, fears).
3. Reflect on your past self.
4. Analyze your current strategies for planning your life.
5. Evaluate how you prioritize and manage your time.
6. Write down your top three takeaways from each chapter (part one).
7. Write down any questions and discuss them with your mentor, sponsor, or coach.

PART TWO

WHAT IS YOUR STRATEGY FOR THE FUTURE?

What Is Your Strategy for the Future?

Strategic future planning means making a conscious effort to plan activities during your life. It involves identifying early on what "success" means to you and how to strategize your purpose in life, a.k.a. your *why*. Finding your *why* is basically finding the reason you think you are put on this Earth, based on *your* uniqueness.

There will be no one else like you—ever!

This simple fact should prompt each of us to ask ourselves a few basic questions.

What wakes you up in the morning?

Why do you think you are here?

What were you born to do?

Having a clear understanding of your purpose will lead to greater fulfillment, growth, financial stability, and occupational awareness. Continuous process improvement should also be a part of your strategic future planning, as it helps you adapt to changing circumstances and stay relevant in your chosen field.

As we continue, let's consider a few more questions; your answers will help to determine where you stand now and where you'd like to go.

What Does Success Mean in Our Culture and Society?

Depending on which culture or society we come from or are a part of now, this may prompt different responses. It also depends on your generation, gender, race, and religion, not to mention your economic background and the opportunities that may be available.

In our culture/society here in the US, success for a woman

means having an education, working for a living, taking care of our spouses and children, and sometimes even taking care of our aging parents. Success could mean financial independence to do what we want whenever we want. It can also mean personal achievement in mastering a skill or doing something meaningful.

However, when we are in a culture that measures or attributes success that is not aligned with our own values, it may bring us professional success but feel like a personal failure. For example, an individual forced to finish a degree in business because that is what their family wanted them to do may be successful externally, but if they wanted to be an artist instead, they are not fulfilling their internal passion but rather their family's pressure.

My mom's response was unique to her experience. When I asked her about the meaning of success, her answer was based on her generation of baby boomers in the Philippines. To her, success meant not having to work, being able to stay home, and playing mahjong with her friends. For the men in her life, success meant having a car and house, providing for family, including in-laws, and kids playing freely with their neighbors with no television or cell phones.

What Does Having Purpose Really Mean, and How Does It Vary from Person to Person?

Having a purpose means aligning what makes you unique, based on your talents and what you enjoy doing. This varies from person to person because we all come from different backgrounds and experiences. Our families are different, and we all come from different cultural and racial backgrounds. Although there are similarities, we are all special.

How Do We Measure Improvement?

There are several ways to measure improvements. One that I have been teaching is based on SMART goals. Goal-setting has to be specific, measurable, attainable, relevant, and timebound. Based on this, you can incrementally measure improvements over time. For example, if your goal is to lose weight, you may state clearly and unequivocally, "I want to lose five pounds in three months."

How Can We Measure Our Adaptive Skills?

There are several ways we can measure our adaptive skills. We can conduct self-assessments and request feedback from others, depending on what adaptive skills we are working on. For example, if we are working on adaptive skills at a personal level at home, we can ask those who live with us, such as our spouses, roommates, or children, for feedback. If we are working on adaptive skills in the workplace, we can ask leaders, colleagues, and coworkers for feedback.

CHAPTER 6

The Arc of Improvement

It's time to explore the conscious efforts you must make in planning your activities during your life. These include identifying early what success means to you, fulfillment (an essential component of strategic future planning), growth (another critical component of strategic future planning), financial stability, occupational awareness, and continuous process improvement.

CONSCIOUS EFFORT

Strategic future planning means taking time to think about your goals, dreams, and aspirations and developing a plan to achieve them. Without a plan, it is easy to get distracted or lose focus on what is important, leading to a sense of aimlessness.

As I previously stated, when I was younger, everything I had to do was dictated by someone else. When I was very young, my father had a schedule for me and my sister, which dictated from morning until evening what we had to do, ranging from required reading to what chores we had to helping our grandmother around the house. In school, from the first bell to the last, our schedule was based on going from one classroom to another. When I first joined the military, our schedule was based on what training or tasks we needed to get done daily. As I became more senior, I had more autonomy with my schedule, but when I got married and had children, it was necessary for me to manage my time more effectively because other people depended on me.

As I observe different people and leaders, it's been interesting to see how each one manages their time. I also recognize that, regardless of how many years they have been in the military, it's baffling that some colleagues who are about to retire don't know what they are going to do upon retirement.

I have also seen different people in the military who did not know how to manage their careers. This is when I started to realize that I had to make a conscious effort to strategically plan my future way in advance and then plan backward from that future point. I also realized that I had to figure out what was important to me and what my values were for them to align with what I wanted to accomplish in the future. I also found that the people I was mentoring did not have a system in place to accomplish this for themselves or did not know how to do so.

THE MEANING OF SUCCESS

Identifying early what success means to you means answering this question: what is your *why*? This indicates your purpose in life, and it guides nearly all your decisions and actions. Without a clear understanding of your *why*, it is difficult to stay focused and motivated to achieve your goals. Take the time to reflect on your values, passions, and strengths to determine what success means to you.

Depending on one's gender, culture, and economic or racial background, everyone has unique perspectives about their w*hy*. Without a clear eye on *why*, it makes it difficult to figure out what's important to you and to determine your values. It is also difficult to articulate to other people who may be trying to help you or who are affected by your decisions when you don't take the time to figure out what's important to you early on.

Figuring out your *why* is a major building block, and you cannot move to the next block until you complete it. It doesn't matter how many tasks you accomplish. If they are not aligned with what you're passionate about, it will not matter what tasks those are, certainly not in the long run. Nobody else can do this for you because this is a personal thing that *you* must determine for yourself!

FULFILLMENT

Fulfillment is an essential component of strategic future planning. It involves living a life that is aligned with your values, passions, and purpose. When you are fulfilled, you are more likely to feel a sense of satisfaction and contentment with your life, which can lead to greater happiness and well-being.

When I reflect on all the things I have done so far in my life, I feel fulfilled because they are aligned with my values, passion, and purpose. My fulfillment comes from helping other people and figuring out how they can help themselves. I also feel a sense of satisfaction and contentment in making sure that those around me are set up for success. I involve those important people in my decision-making so my fulfillment is not mine alone. It also includes those who are affected by my decisions——at home and at work.

GROWTH

Growth is another critical component of strategic future planning. It involves constantly learning and developing new skills and knowledge to adapt to changing circumstances while remaining relevant in your chosen field. When you prioritize growth, you are better equipped to achieve your goals and reach your full potential.

I joined the Army when I was seventeen years old. During that time, I was already proficient in maintaining a task list. I was very good at sports, which help me not only because of the competitiveness but also in teamwork, listening skills, and executing instructions. When I joined the military, it was required for me to work with other soldiers and be physically active, and being part of youth sports teams made this process relatively seamless.

I continually sought out opportunities for growth to keep me going in my career when I joined the military. Most of the people in my high school could not believe that I enlisted. Let alone for five years. I became a patient administrator and later found out that I could become a physician assistant, so I applied for that opportunity. I knew that my passion was teaching, and when I retired, I wanted to teach, so I began to work on earning a doctorate in education, which I eventually completed.

Furthermore, I was interested in orthopedics, so when I was given the opportunity to become a PA in orthopedics, I took advantage of it. The military gave me opportunities for different jobs: a researcher in a research institute, an inspector general for a major command, and a commander of a clinic.

Sports helped me figure out some of these processes. It is important to have a growth mindset and flexibility because things change all the time, and the requirements change as well.

I feel very fortunate that I have been able to advance in my career, from being enlisted to becoming an officer, and in my education, applicable to the civilian market and the military.

My deployments have also provided me with opportunities to learn from people with different backgrounds, here and abroad, not only from the Department of Defense but also from our North Atlantic Treaty Organization allies.

FINANCIAL STABILITY

Financial stability is an essential consideration in strategic future planning. It involves creating a financial plan that supports your goals and aspirations, including saving for retirement, paying off debt, and investing in your future. When you have financial stability, you are less likely to be stressed and can focus on pursuing your passions and achieving your goals.

In the US, I lived with my mother, then a single parent, and she had four children. She held three to four jobs at a time. We were unable to go on lavish vacations or spend money on material things. When other classmates planned for a ski trip, I did not think, *Why can't I go?*

It was not something I was concerned about because my mother had to make ends meet on her own—and that was that. She missed a lot of our activities, such as sporting events and school award ceremonies, but she never missed feeding us, taking care of us, or loving us.

Toward the end of high school, she told me and my sister that she did not have enough money for us to go to college. My sister and I looked for recruiters to join the military, and we settled on the Army. We both went to basic training and advanced individual training.

Around November of that year, my sister was on leave and called me at my first duty station to tell me our brother Luis died. I went home and saw my sister, who told me she had been able to save more than $2,000 while in basic and advanced individual training. I, on the other hand, wasted all my money at Fort Sam Houston at the Hacienda, basically a place where trainees hung out. I spent my money on frivolous things, like popcorn and sodas.

I learned my lesson and started saving. I also started planning better for what I wanted to spend my money on: my education, a car, and a house. When I left my first duty station, I had already finished an associate's degree and saved enough money to put a down payment on a condo. My second duty station team was really surprised because they said they had officers who did not even have as much money as I did, and I was, a mere specialist.

I learned from my grandmother that it was important to own real estate, so throughout my career, whenever we moved from one location to another, we bought a home that was affordable for a mid-level, noncommissioned officer. Whenever we left a duty station, we kept the home as a rental property. When we moved to another duty station, we purchased another home and were still able to pay for the rental property if it was temporarily without tenants. Although we are now downsizing our real estate properties, for a time, we owned five homes and only had to rent a home once. (We lived on post once because it was mandatory.) We have paid for our children's education through 529 plans and maintaining TSP and Roth IRAs for our retirement.

Financial independence is one of our big rocks.

OCCUPATIONAL AWARENESS

Occupational awareness involves understanding your strengths, weaknesses, and interests and how they align with your career aspirations. When you have occupational awareness, you are better able to make informed decisions about your career path, including choosing a job that is a good fit for you and developing the skills and knowledge needed to advance in your field.

It was always important to me to be able to survive in the military and as a civilian. As a military PA, I am required to be certified, including taking certification exams and completing continuing medical education requirements. When the civilian sector has changes in the profession, it affects the military. This is why it's important to know what the requirements are in your field. This often requires time to complete certain education and certification requirements.

CONTINUOUS PROCESS IMPROVEMENT

Continuous process improvement (CPI) is a critical component of strategic future planning. It involves regularly reflecting on your progress and identifying areas for improvement. When you prioritize CPI, you can adapt to changing circumstances and stay motivated to achieve your goals. It helps you develop a growth mindset, which is essential for success.

I was able to complete certification for the highest level of Lean Six Sigma, the master black belt. I help others with their certification requirements, which is helpful in the military sector *and* civilian sector. CPI is important because you identify things that can be improved, based on decreasing cost, improving quality, and increasing speed.

Q&A with Nicole Baker

Nicole is a nurse with a focus on patient safety and health-care quality. She has more than seventeen years of experience in the nursing field. She is proud of being a servant leader with the leadership ability to foster partnerships. She has received many accolades, including being chosen as "Nurse of the Year" at one of the largest Army health clinics, along with project recognition from the Army surgeon general's initiatives.

Q: You are so accomplished in your professional field. How has this carried over into your personal life?

A: You would think that with all the great experience I've had, I would be well-versed in time management, planning, and prioritization, but I still have a lot of room for growth, both at work and at home.

Q: What is your biggest challenge in this area?

A: I love building sustainable relationships, but I am lacking when it comes to building one with myself and truly understanding time management. I am a self-starter who thrives on inspiring and supporting others, going above and beyond, and paying it forward. Prioritizing others over myself can often interfere with my time management.

Q: What other areas are you struggling to improve?

A: Planning for the future, time management, and prioritization.

CHAPTER 7

Evaluate Your Current State of Self

Here, we reflect on your past self and appreciate what you have done so far. We examine how you currently plan your future, prioritize, and manage your time. We will determine what is working and what is not working and what your biggest challenges are.

When it comes to planning your future, it's essential to start by understanding your current self. That means clearly and honestly understanding who you are right now, including your strengths, weaknesses, values, passions, and goals. This process is essential for planning your future. By understanding who you are right now and what you want to achieve, you can create a strategic plan that aligns with your values, passions, and goals. Regular self-assessment and feedback from others can help you stay on track and adjust as needed, ensuring that you continue to grow and thrive as you move forward.

When I look back on my childhood, my favorite memories were with my maternal grand aunt, Marcela (I affectionately called her *Apu Celang*), when she took me to school with her. She was a third-grade teacher. I would sit on her desk, looking at her table, where she had pictures of my brothers and sister. I recall with fondness the children around me. I was just listening, too young to learn what they were learning.

I was involved in educational environments as early as I can remember. When I moved with my grandmother, we were surrounded by her established fashion and beauty school for women.

My father was a substitute teacher working on his doctorate. He liked to write with his typewriter, and I can still hear the noise it made.

When we moved to the US, I started playing different sports and realized I was pretty good at them. So, I kept playing throughout high school, and during my senior year, I was voted scholar-athlete of the year.

Recalling these memories helps me recount my accomplishments and realize I can be proud of what I did when I was younger. These experiences and milestones helped me become who I am today by forming the building blocks and the foundation to my success and resilience.

YOUR CURRENT SELF

When it comes to planning your future, it's essential to start by understanding yourself. Have a clear understanding of who you are right now, including your strengths, weaknesses, values, passions, and goals. But you can only do this if you honest about how you have arrived here. That means revisiting your past. Take the time to go back to your responses from part one. Reflect on your past self and appreciate what you have done so far. Also, reflect on how you plan your future, prioritize, and manage your time. Determine what is working, not working, and what your biggest challenges are.

This is essential for planning your future. By understanding who you are right now and what you want to achieve, you can create a strategic plan that aligns with your values, passions, and goals. Regular self-assessment and feedback from others can help you stay on track and adjust as needed, ensuring that you continue to grow and thrive.

Q&A with Nicole Baker (Part 2)

Q: How would you assess your ability to plan for the future?

A: I usually define myself as a resilient military spouse, a mother of two boys, with the extreme ability to build everlasting relationships. But when you ask me about where I see myself in five years, no matter how many times I have been asked this question, I really don't have a good answer. As a military spouse, planning for my future is something I don't always have the pleasure of doing.

Q: What is your *why*?

A: What's my *why*? You must ask, then, why am I a nurse? I lost my father in a tragic car accident when I was five years old. He was saving my life. I will always remember the medical staff and how they treated me. The nurses were there for my mother when she had to tell her three small children (ages five, three, and one) that their father wasn't coming home––ever. So, planning for the future, managing my time, and prioritizing those I love is a must. I guess I'm still trying to figure out where I fit in with all these plans.

CHAPTER 8

Reverse Engineer Your Plan

Once you have a clear picture of where you want to be in thirty years, you can start reverse engineering your plan. This means breaking down your goal into smaller, achievable steps that will lead you toward your end goal.

For example, if your end goal is to become a successful entrepreneur in the technology industry, you might start by researching successful entrepreneurs in the field and the steps they took to get there. You might also consider the skills and knowledge you need to develop and the resources and connections you need to acquire along the way.

CREATE A TIMELINE

It is important to think as far into the future as you can. Thirty years seems impossible to most people, but in the blink of an eye, it will pass, and you will look back and ask questions.

"How did I get here?"

"Did I plan well enough?"

"How can I fix my mistakes and lack of planning?"

This is why it's important to write your obituary. If you don't feel comfortable, just think of yourself at ninety, looking back at the things you have done in your life.

What will be your legacy?

What are the things you want your children and grandchildren to remember?

Remember, you are unique and important, with something special to give to the world. You have something meaningful to share with others. What is it? Do you know?

BIG ROCKS AND LITTLE ROCKS

Artwork by Sofia Duran-Stanton

Big rocks symbolize our priorities. They encompass the tasks, projects, or goals each of us must accomplish. They define our mission-critical objectives and do *not* include items on anyone's messy sprawling to-do list.

When you think about where you will be in thirty years, it's okay to write your vision in pencil. Things will change. Remember your responses to finding out what your *ikigai* is made of. You have to figure out your values and what's ultimately important to you in the long run.

What are your big rocks?

Once you figure out where you think you will be in thirty years, plan backward. Figure out where you see yourself in twenty years, your passion, your values, where you want to be, where you want to live, and who you want to live with (if that's the way you choose to do it).

What are your next set of big rocks?

Next, go to ten years from now. What's your passion? What are your values? Where are you? Who are you living with, and why? What are you doing?

What is your next set of big and medium rocks?

From there, you can complete your five-year plan. Consider your ten-, twenty-, and thirty-year plans. They all have to align. Once you reach your five-year plan, it's like you're no longer writing down your thoughts and dreams in pencil. They are becoming more concrete. So, what are you doing? Where are you? Who are you with? What have you accomplished?

What is your next set of big, medium, and little rocks?

If there are certain things you want to do thirty years from now, like retire in Hawaii, that may cost a lot, so you need to start saving as much as you can in order to get there. This is how your five-, ten-, and twenty-year plans connect. How will you start saving now?

As for me, in thirty years, I want to be retired, traveling the world, and still teaching. Therefore, my twenty-year plan must reflect where I will live and travel destinations. My ten-year plan (when I will likely be retired from the military) must include increased savings!

How will I make that happen? Will I still be working despite being retired from the military? If I want to travel, I have to stay active and healthy, ensuring I enjoy my travels.

The last step in the backward method is establishing an annual plan, which may be more visible now. So, instead of just doing an annual plan on an annual basis, you have strategically envisioned your life, your passion, your values, and your big rocks.

Incorporate how your partner and family fit into this backward planning. How are those around you affected? Plan accordingly. After all, most of us are part of a team!

PART TWO

Fundamentals Review and Workbook Preview

As you continue your path to finding your *ikigai* and making it a viable and winning part of your life, do you need to reconsider your answers?

A PERSONAL ASSESSMENT

1. What does "success" mean to you?
2. What *is* your *why*?
3. How are you strategizing your purpose in life, a.k.a., your "*why*"?
4. What makes you unique?
5. How do you measure improvement?
6. How do you measure your adaptive skills?
7. What conscious efforts do you make in planning your daily activities?
8. Are you living a life that is aligned with your values, passions, and purpose?
9. Do you have financial stability, and if not, what is your plan to achieve it?
10. How would you rate your occupational awareness?

EXERCISES AND TAKEAWAYS

1. What are your big rocks in life?
2. What are your thirty-year big rocks?
3. What are your twenty-year big rocks?
4. What are your ten-year big rocks?
5. What are your five-year big rocks?
6. What are your annual big rocks?
7. What are your daily big rocks?
8. What are your top three key takeaways from each chapter (part two)?

PART THREE

HOW DO YOU PRIORITIZE?

How Do You Prioritize?

Prioritization is the key to effective strategic life planning. Without it, you may find yourself overwhelmed with too many tasks and not enough time to accomplish them all. Prioritization helps you focus on the most important things in your life and ensures that you're using your time and resources effectively.

It's all about big rocks (BR) and little rocks (LR).

By defining your big picture, long-term goals (big rocks) and your daily short-term goals (little rocks), you can learn how to prioritize and achieve them to live a purposeful and fulfilling life.

When I first started doing BR/LR assessments, I did it in December to prepare for the new year. I soon discovered that I was missing out on advanced planning by not preparing early enough for the new fiscal year that starts in October. Therefore, I moved my annual assessments to September so I could prepare for the fiscal year starting in October. I also still do it in December to prepare for the new calendar year.

I still review my list every quarter to see if anything major needs to be adjusted. I also use a monthly tracker of events for the whole year, where I include the big rocks/little rocks I carry so I can see if I am on track.

I cannot stress enough the importance of prioritization in strategic life planning. In part three, you will find tips and tools on how to prioritize your life, and the perspective of big rocks and little rocks will play a major role in this process.

CHAPTER 9

Why? How? What?

The Golden Circle is a concept developed by Simon Oliver Sinek that explains how great leaders and organizations inspire others.[1] Sinek, age fifty, is an English-born American author and inspirational speaker. He is the author of five books, including *Start with Why* (2009) and *The Infinite Game* (2019). He has devoted his life to sharing his thinking and leading a movement to inspire people to do the things that inspire them. Simon may be best known for popularizing the concept of WHY in his first Ted Talk in 2009. It has since become one of the most-watched talks of all time on TED.com, with more than thirty-seven million views.

The Golden Circle consists of three concentric circles: the "Why" in the center, surrounded by the "How," and finally the "What."[2] The Golden Circle emphasizes the importance of purpose-driven leadership and encourages organizations to focus on their beliefs and values to drive success.[3]

The Golden Circle provides compelling evidence of how much (more) we can achieve if everything we do begins by asking a simple question: "Why?"[4]

This process creates order and predictability in human behavior. Put simply, the Golden Circle helps us understand why we do what we do.

---

[1]. Simon Sinek, "Simon Sinek," July 24, 2024, accessed July 24, 2024, https://simonsinek.com/golden-circle/.
[2] Ibid.
[3] Ibid.
[4] Ibid.

Sinek argues that most organizations focus on what they do rather than *why* they do it and that this approach does not inspire others.[5] Instead, he suggests that by starting with why, organizations can create a sense of purpose that inspires others to follow and act.[6]

The Golden Circle emphasizes the importance of purpose-driven leadership and encourages organizations to focus on their beliefs and values to drive success.[7]

Sinek's common example for the Golden Circle is Apple. He explains that rather than describing Apple as a company that makes computers, they position themselves as a company that challenges the status quo and does things differently.

For me, my *why* is to continue to be someone who provides education to others by teaching or mentoring. Since this is my purpose, my *how* is teaching and mentoring. A *what* for me comes through this book and creating courses. This is also one of the reasons *why* I decided to pursue a doctorate in education; I am passionate about teaching and educating.

The same sensibilities apply to our personal lives. Starting with why is crucial when it comes to strategic future planning. Understanding your purpose and motivation for the things you want to achieve can help guide your decision-making and prioritize your goals. Your *why* is the driving force behind your actions and should be at the forefront when planning your future.

My *why* is helping others see themselves achieve their best selves and empowering them in finding ways they, too, can find their why, by strategically planning for their future, learning to prioritize, and managing their time.

> What is your *why*?
>
> What is your purpose?
>
> How do you get after your *why*?

---

[5] Ibid.
[6] Ibid.
[7] Ibid.

What do you do now?

What should you be doing?

Q&A with Michelle Patterson

Michelle Patterson, fifty-three, a retired Army veteran and mother of one, struggled without a concrete strategy when she transitioned to a new job back in Texas. While she could control the packing and moving, she was behind when it came to feeling calm in her life.

Q: What are your thoughts about strategic future planning?

A: I plan to work for the Veterans Administration in three to five years as a retired Army veteran. I just realized that not planning for the future affects people's health and well-being.

Q: What is working well in your future planning?

A: Packing and moving back to Texas for a new job.

Q: What is currently *not* working well?

A: Not having a strategy.

Q: What is your biggest challenge when it comes to future planning?

A: Things I want to do don't align with jobs, so I am reactive instead of proactive on a day-to-day basis. I'm always behind, stressed, and working hard, with no personal life.

Q: How do you feel about not having done the planning (future, time, career)?

A: Frustrated and challenged, like a punch in the gut. It's been a huge setback, and it sucks because I don't feel good. I'm often stressed, sad, and depressed.

Q: What have you tried already?

A: Close out notes. Balance more time with my patients with less notes or less time with patients and more time for notes.

Q: Why didn't it work? What was your investment?

A: I was tired and exhausted.

Q: Why is it important to you to solve this challenge?

A: It will reduce my stress, take away depression, and decrease my anxiety at work.

Q: What does your ideal situation look like?

A: Wake up, travel, enjoy work, be proactive, teach, write, publish, and do my shopping business. I always say, "Happy provider, happy patients."

Q: How will you know when you have achieved your goal?

A: When I'm not working seven days a week, when my patients feel taken care of, when I'm happy, and when I can enjoy working, writing, and publishing.

Q: When you achieve your goals, what will you be able to do?

A: Help veterans and my community and work at the homeless shelter.

Q: What would your life look like if this problem was gone?

A: Wonderful! I'd be happy. I'd have time to work out, travel, and see family and friends.

CHAPTER 10

Conducting a SWOT Analysis

SWOT stands for strengths, weaknesses, opportunities, and threats. A SWOT analysis is useful for future planning as you assess your current state and identify areas for improvement.

Strengths refer to the positive aspects of your current situation, such as skills, resources, and relationships, that can help you achieve your goals. My strengths are time management, networking, prioritization, punctuality, and cultural diversity.

Weaknesses are areas that need improvement, such as a lack of skills, limited resources, or negative relationships that can hinder your progress. My weaknesses are the following: I am harder on myself than I am on others. I expect others to perform at the same or higher level than me, which may not be feasible. I am a naturally introverted/forcibly extroverted person, so I sometimes have difficulty communicating. I like to get things done quickly, but sometimes I lack the patience needed to wait, depending on who I am working with and how they operate.

Opportunities are external factors, such as emerging trends, new technologies, or potential partnerships, that you can use to help you achieve your goals. I value different opportunities to collaborate with new people in new areas and with new communities.

Threats are external factors that can negatively impact your progress, such as competition, economic downturns, or changing regulations. For me, threats are our global adversaries, technological shutdowns, and regulations and policies that must be followed.

A SWOT analysis is a useful tool in strategic future planning, as it helps you assess your current state and identify areas for improvement. You can identify your strengths and opportunities to leverage, as well as your weaknesses and threats to address. This can help you create a plan for action that will move you toward your desired future state.

Start by identifying your strengths and weaknesses. This is an internal process that involves self-inspection and deep reflection, and it's only worthwhile if you are honest with yourself! Then look externally to identify your opportunities and threats.

I learned SWOT analysis from my time in the military, and I have used it to assess myself personally and professionally as I review my job or position. I also use it as a tool when mentoring others. I use personal assessments to let them see themselves, and they share it with those they trust to give them a 360-degree assessment.

A professional SWOT analysis is valuable. I have used it to help individuals personally and professionally and to help organizations based on collective SWOT analyses from different people inside their teams.

Since we previously discussed backward planning, now is the time to conceptualize your responses from parts one and two and review your SWOT analysis. This is the time to be more specific and answer questions about your long-term planning.

When you have your long-term and midterm plans, you can determine your short-term, annual plan. Now is the time to be more decisive.

Utilize **PDCA**: **P**lan. **D**o. Check. Act. PDCA is a four-step process in an effective continuous process improvement in acting on changes.

CHAPTER 11

The 7 Habits of Highly Effective People

The late Stephen Covey developed a path for planning and accomplishing one's goals. He encapsulated the effort into seven habits. The seven habits of highly effective people are essential for future strategic planning, prioritization, and time management, especially for women, as they provide a framework for personal and professional growth.[8]

The habits encourage women to take responsibility for their lives, define their goals, prioritize their tasks, communicate effectively, build meaningful relationships, collaborate with others, and continuously improve themselves.

By applying these habits to their lives, women can develop the necessary skills, mindsets, and habits to achieve their long-term vision, maximize their potential, and live a fulfilling and balanced life.

Here are tangible tools you can use to prepare for your planning.

Habit 1: Be proactive.

Don't let life just happen to you. Take charge of the aspects you can control. This is why it is important to be proactive in finding your *ikigai*, knowing your values and your SWOT personally and professionally. Be proactive in learning how your actions affect those close to you. Identify those who can help you in being or becoming your best self.

---

[8] Stephen Covey, The 7 Habits of Highly Effective People (New York: Simon and Schuster, 1989).

Habit 2: Begin with the end in mind and create a career timeline that takes into consideration key components for the future.

Write your obituary. Where do you see yourself in thirty years? Consider your age, education, military education, positions, and where you want to go. Do this with your spouse and children as well.

Habit 3: Put first things first and think of big rocks and little rocks.

We've explored the concept of BR and LR and why it is essential to identify them when planning your life, including your passion, family, career, friendship, and actions.

Knowing your big rocks means knowing your priorities and long-term goals. Now is the time to revisit your responses. What is your *ikigai*? What is your *why*? What are your values? Perhaps you have new ideas to add.

One of my big rocks is my career and success, whether in the military or as a civilian. Part of this is teaching. I knew that I needed a PhD to do what I wanted in the education field, and I also wanted it!

When it comes to LR, knowing your short-term goals and tasks is essential.

In line with my career example, my earlier short-term goals were to earn an associate degree, then a bachelor's, followed by a master's and a doctorate in education.

However, there may be times when your big rocks may not align with what you need for your short-term goals. For example, someone may have a passion for baking, and one of their big rocks may be to open a bakery when they retire.

Meanwhile, a short-term goal may be earning money in their current job as a medical assistant, which requires them to take courses in the short-term to maintain their qualification, but they also need to save money and learn how to bake for their long-term bakery goal. They reach that long-term goal incrementally in the short-term as much as they can while still earning money as a medical assistant.

Their dream of owning a bakery will not be possible until they have the funds and skills as a baker and business owner.

When you're planning your life, it is essential to identify your BR. These are the things that matter most to you. They will bring you the most happiness and fulfillment. Once you've identified them, you can identify your little rocks. These daily tasks and activities fill your time but are less important.

My BR are spending time with family, financial independence, leaving a legacy of helping others become their best selves, and learning from other cultures by traveling the world.

My little rocks are attending meetings, writing, saving, planning my travels, and attending courses.

Achieving balance in your life means finding a way to fit in your big rocks and LR while achieving your goals and living a fulfilling life. This requires careful planning and time management. Schedule time for your big rocks first and then fit in your little rocks.

BR will fill up most of your jar of life, and the little rocks fill empty spaces. If you fill your jar of life with LR first, the BR will not fit and may even fall out.

Habit 4: Think win-win.

This is a crucial mindset for women. This habit emphasizes the importance of seeking mutual benefit and looking for solutions that are advantageous for everyone involved.

When women approach their personal and professional lives with a win-win mindset, they are more likely to find sustainable solutions and build positive relationships. This habit encourages women to collaborate and find ways to create value for themselves and others, leading to greater success and fulfillment in their lives.

Win-win also means listening and considering feedback from those affected by our decisions, such as partners or children.

Habit 5: Seek first to understand, then to be understood.

This habit emphasizes listening and understanding before communicating our ideas. It encourages building strong relationships and effective communication skills.

It also incorporates your SWOT analysis results. I have difficulty articulating and communicating with others. Knowing this is a weakness, I must make a more conscious effort to talk to the people affected by my decisions. I can incorporate one of my strengths, planning in advance when I can talk to my loved ones about what is happening in my life and theirs.

Habit 6: Synergize.

This habit emphasizes teamwork and cooperation to achieve greater results. Synergizing involves finding creative solutions to problems by working collaboratively with others, being open-minded to diverse perspectives, and leveraging the strengths of each team member.

It is important for women to practice this habit, as it can lead to better communication, stronger relationships, and more effective problem-solving.

Synergizing with loved ones affected by my decisions will incorporate not just my ideas but theirs as well, which also touches on habit 4.

One of my big rocks is spending time with family and talking to them about my future plans (BR). Our weekly meetings also get after our little rocks.

Habit 7: Sharpen the saw.

This habit emphasizes self-renewal and self-care. Sharpening the saw means regularly engaging in activities that improve physical, emotional, mental, and spiritual well-being. These include exercise, meditation, reading, and hobbies.

I sharpen the saw in several ways. I exercise regularly. This touches my big rocks and little rocks. Since traveling is one of my big rocks, I have to exercise to maintain my endurance as I age. Exercise also helps with my military requirements in passing the Army Combat Fitness Test and the physical and mental rigors of daily activities at work.

I also enjoy reading self-help books. This gets after one of my big rocks, helping others, because I am learning different perspectives. Reading also activates my mind.

Q&A with Maria Delgado (from the intro)

Q: What are your thoughts about strategic future planning?

A: I am currently working on a PhD. I plan three to six months in advance, and I want to plan now for when I am sixty-five to seventy.

Q: What is currently working well in your future planning?

A: Just thinking about the process of planning my future.

Q: What is currently *not* working well?

A: I sometimes upset my family and friends by being anal about plans, and I worry about my plan not being achievable.

Q: What is your biggest challenge when it comes to future planning?

A: My family, helping people who are relying on me, aging, and overwhelm.

Q: How do you feel about not having done the planning (future, time, career)?

A: It's a problem missing out on things I could be doing by not being organized, and neglecting important things causes anxiety.

Q: What have you tried already?

A: Taking family back to their home, and no more spending money!

Q: Why didn't it work? What was your investment?

A: I lost money and time.

Q: Why is it important to you to solve this challenge?

A: It's for my sense of being, my health, and my financial fitness.

Q: What does your ideal situation look like?

A: Less spending, less stress, taking care of myself, and having peace of mind.

Q: How will you know when you have achieved your goal?

A: I won't be going back and forth to New York for family.

Q: When you achieve your goals, what will you be able to do?

A: Save for retirement and pay for retirement and school.

Q: What would your life look like if this problem was gone?

A: I will keep up with school and not worry all the time.

CHAPTER 12

Prioritization Tools

Prioritization tools can be helpful for women in strategic future planning because they provide practical methods for evaluating and prioritizing tasks and activities based on their value and impact, enabling more efficient use of time and resources.

The Worth-Your-Time Test

This is a tool for assessing the value of a task or activity by asking whether it aligns with your goals and values and whether it will have a significant impact on your life.

The Red Amber Green (RAG) Rating System

This tool is for evaluating tasks and projects based on their progress or completion status, with tasks being classified as red (not started or behind schedule), amber (in progress but not yet complete), or green (completed or on track).

The Getting Things Done (GTD) Method

This comprehensive approach to task management and productivity is focused on capturing all tasks and ideas, organizing them into a system, and regularly reviewing and completing them.

The Pareto Analysis

This is also known as the 80/20 rule, which suggests that 20 percent of efforts can result in 80 percent of outcomes, which can be used to identify the most impactful tasks and activities to focus on.

These prioritization tools can be helpful for women in strategic future planning. They provide practical methods for evaluating and prioritizing tasks and activities based on their value and impact, enabling a more efficient use of time and resources. *Failing to plan is planning to fail.*

PART THREE

Fundamentals Review and Workbook Preview

A PERSONAL ASSESSMENT

1. What are your big rocks and little rocks?
2. What is your *why*?
3. What is your purpose?
4. How do you get after your *why*?
5. What do you do now?
6. What should you be doing?
7. What are your most effective habits?
8. What are your most ineffective habits?
9. How would you rate yourself when it comes to prioritizing?
10. How could you improve?

EXERCISES AND TAKEAWAYS

1. Draw your own Golden Circle.
2. Do your own SWOT analysis (strengths, weaknesses, opportunities, and threats).
3. If you could ask yourself one honest question, what would it be?
4. Incorporate each of the seven habits in your life.
5. Try each of the prioritization tools and see which ones work best for you.
6. What are your top three takeaways from each chapter (part four)?

PART 4

CAN YOU MANAGE YOUR TIME?

Can You Manage Your Time?

Time is our most valuable commodity. There are seven days in a week and twenty-four hours in a day. A year has twelve months, fifteen weeks, or three hundred and sixty-five days. We all have the same amount of time, so learning how to manage it is crucial to *everything*.

Artwork by Sofia Duran-Stanton

Managing free time effectively is important for personal well-being and productivity. Here are some general strategies, along with examples of how women can implement them:

1. Set clear goals.

Set daily goals for yourself, such as completing a certain number of work tasks and spending quality time with family. This helps prioritize your time and stay on track.

2. Prioritize self-care.

Dedicate a portion of your free time to self-care activities like exercise, meditation, and reading. This rejuvenates and improves overall well-being.

3. Time block.

Use time blocking to allocate specific time slots for different tasks. For instance, designate one hour for email, two hours for deep work, and an hour for socializing.

4. Limit distractions.

Turn off your phone's notifications and set specific periods for checking social media. This will minimize distractions and allow you to focus better during work and personal activities.

5. Learn something new.

Spend your free time learning new skills. Take online courses in subjects you are passionate about, which enriches your knowledge and gives you a sense of accomplishment.

6. Spend quality time with loved ones.

If you value family time, schedule regular outings with your children or significant other. This strengthens bonds and creates cherished memories.

7. Volunteer and give back.

Dedicate some of your free time to volunteering at a local charity. This can give you a sense of purpose and fulfillment.

8. Plan ahead.

Plan your free time in advance, whether it's scheduling movie nights with friends or setting aside time for hobbies. This helps you make the most of your available time.

9. Delegate and outsource.

Occasionally delegate household chores and tasks to your family members, allowing you to focus on your career and personal development.

10. Be flexible and adaptable.

Be adaptable with your free time. Maintain a to-do list but remain open to spontaneity and enjoy seizing unexpected opportunities.

Remember, the key to effective time management is finding a balance that works for you personally. It's about aligning your daily activities with your goals and values to ensure a fulfilling and well-rounded life.

DO!

1. Define your short-term and long-term goals to stay focused.
2. Identify high-priority tasks and tackle them first.
3. Allocate specific time blocks for different activities.
4. Delegate tasks to others.

5. Schedule short breaks to recharge and stay productive.
6. Politely decline tasks that don't align with your goals.
7. Utilize productivity apps and tools to streamline tasks.
8. Create daily, weekly, and monthly schedules to stay organized.
9. Group similar activities to minimize context-switching.
10. Regularly assess your time management strategies and make necessary adjustments.

DON'T!

1. Procrastinate.
2. Overcommit.
3. Multitask unnecessarily. Focus on one task at a time to increase efficiency.
4. Ignore self-care. Neglecting self-care can lead to burnout; make time for it.
5. Micromanage. Trust others to handle tasks without constant supervision.
6. Let distractions rule. Minimize interruptions and distractions.
7. Fail to set boundaries. Establish boundaries to protect your time.
8. Waste time on low-value activities. Be selective about how you spend your time.
9. Rush through tasks. Quality is often more important than speed.
10. Neglect personal growth. Allocate time for learning and self-improvement.

These guidelines can help women effectively manage their time and achieve their personal and professional goals.

CHAPTER 13

How to Write SMART Goals

SMART stands for **s**pecific, **m**easurable, **a**chievable, **r**elevant, and time-bound.

This means that the goals we set should be *specific*.

We need to have a clear understanding of what is to be accomplished and a *measurable* means of quantifying and tracking our progress.

Our goals must be *achievable*, with realistic expectations and available resources.

They must be *relevant* to our overall plan and vision.

They also must be *time-bound*, with a specific deadline for completion.

Having SMART goals allows women to stay focused on their goals, track their progress, and prioritize their time and efforts toward what matters most.

SMART goals provide a roadmap for women to reach their desired outcomes efficiently and effectively while maintaining a healthy work-life balance.

Let's look at multiple ways they can be relevant to our lives.

SMART GOAL #1: CAREER ADVANCEMENT

Specific: "I want to advance my career by obtaining a leadership position."

Measurable: "I will measure my progress by tracking the number of leadership development courses I complete, the positive feedback I receive from colleagues, and the number of successful CPI initiatives I lead."

Achievable: "I will enhance my skills through training, gain additional experience in CPI, and actively seek out leadership opportunities within the organization."

Relevant: "This goal aligns with my career aspirations and the organization's growth plans, making it a relevant and valuable pursuit."

Time-Bound: "I aim to achieve this leadership position within the next two years, allowing me a specific timeframe to work toward this goal."

SMART GOAL #2: IMPROVE TIME MANAGEMENT SKILLS IN SIX MONTHS

Specific: "I want to become more efficient in managing my time and reduce daily distractions to achieve a better work-life balance."

Measurable: "I will measure my progress by tracking the number of completed tasks each day, the reduction in time spent on nonproductive activities, and the increase in the number of hours I spend on self-care and personal development."

Achievable: "I will achieve this by adopting time management techniques, setting boundaries for distractions, and seeking guidance or training as needed."

Relevant: "This goal is relevant as it will help me improve my overall well-being, focus on self-improvement, and excel in both my personal and professional life."

Time-Bound: "I aim to significantly improve my time management skills within the next six months, with regular assessments and adjustments to my strategies along the way."

SMART GOAL #3: IMPROVE PRIORITIZATION SKILLS IN ONE MONTH

Specific: "I want to enhance my ability to prioritize tasks effectively to ensure that I focus on the most important and impactful activities in my daily life."

Measurable: "I will measure my progress by maintaining a daily list of tasks, assigning priority levels to each task, and completing at least 80 percent of high-priority tasks each day."

Achievable: "I will achieve this by learning prioritization techniques, time blocking, and eliminating time-wasting activities."

Relevant: "It will help me maximize my productivity and make better use of my time, allowing me to achieve my personal and professional goals more efficiently."

Time-Bound: "I aim to see a significant improvement in my prioritization skills within the next month, with daily assessments and adjustments to my prioritization strategies."

SMART GOAL #4: IMPROVE TWO-MILE RUN TIME IN FOUR MONTHS

Specific: "I want to enhance my running performance by decreasing my two-mile run time from nineteen minutes to fifteen minutes in four months."

Measurable: "I will measure my progress by timing my two-mile runs regularly and recording my times to track the reduction in time over the four-month period."

Achievable: "I will achieve this by following a structured training plan, including speed workouts, interval training, and consistent running to build endurance and speed."

Relevant: "This goal is relevant because the run is required in the

Army Combat Fitness Test, and it is my weakest event. It also contributes to my overall fitness and helps me push my physical limits while working toward a specific time target."

Time-Bound: "I aim to accomplish this goal within four months, with monthly milestones and regular training assessments to ensure I'm on track."

Q&A with Juana Castillo (from the intro)

Q: What are your thoughts about strategic future planning?

A: I am working on a master's degree for the next two years and am currently in a new position.

Q: What is currently working well in your future planning?

A: Getting support from my husband, having a less stressful job, working close to home, and being healthy.

Q: What is currently *not* working well?

A: I have anxiety about school. I am not good at technology. I don't know what's coming. My mentors are far away.

Q: What is your biggest challenge when it comes to future planning?

A: Time management and choosing whether to prioritize health or work.

Q: How do you feel about not having done the planning (future, time, career)?

A: It's a problem missing out on things I could be doing, not being organized, and neglecting important things, which causes anxiety.

Q: What have you tried already?
A: Involving my husband more in decision-making and asking for help.

Q: What does your ideal situation look like?
A: Life with less stress.

Q: How will you know when you have achieved your goal?
A: When I feel happy and find another challenge.

Q: When you achieve your goals, what will you be able to do?
A: Hold down a six-figure job, make more money for investments, and have a business.

Q: What would your life look like if this problem was gone?
A: I would retire, stay home, and spend more time with my children, and I would have a business of my own wherever I choose.

CHAPTER 14

Tools to Help You Manage Time

There are several ideas, tools, and concepts you can use to manage your time effectively. They include the following: the Eisenhower Matrix, Monkey management, eat the frog, The Pickle Jar Theory, time blocking, the Pomodoro Technique, Parkinson's law, mind mapping, the ABC Method, time audit, and digital detox.

These tools and concepts come from a variety of sources, including time management experts, authors, and common practices, and they have proven valuable for improving productivity.

ACCORDING TO IKE

Dwight D. Eisenhower, the 34th president of the US, who served two terms from 1953 to 1961, was remarkably productive. He was a five-star general in the US Army and supreme commander of the Allied forces in Europe during World War II and throughout his presidency.[9] He launched programs that led to the development of America's interstate highway system, the internet (DARPA), exploration of space (NASA), and the peaceful use of alternative energy sources (Atomic Energy Act).[10] He also served as President of Columbia University and became the first Supreme Commander of NATO. Just to show that he could find balance in his life, he pursued hobbies like golf and oil painting.

---

[9] Clear, James. 2024. How to be More Productive and Eliminate Time Wasting Activities by Using the "Eisenhower Box". Accessed July 24, 2024. https://jamesclear.com/eisenhower-box.
[10] Ibid.

Eisenhower had an incredible ability to sustain his productivity for weeks, months, and years. His methods have been studied by many people.

His most famous productivity strategy is the Eisenhower Box (or Eisenhower Matrix), a simple decision-making tool for being more productive. His strategy for acting and organizing tasks is also simple. Using the decision matrix below, you can separate your actions based on four possibilities.

1. Urgent and important (tasks you will do immediately).
2. Important but not urgent (tasks you will schedule to do later).
3. Urgent but not important (tasks you will delegate to someone else).
4. Neither urgent nor important (tasks that you will eliminate).

This matrix can be used for broad productivity plans ("How should I spend my time each week?") and for smaller, daily plans ("What should I do today?").

Artwork by Sofia Duran-Stanton

Urgent tasks are things you feel you need to react to, such as emails, phone calls, texts, and news stories. Important tasks are things that can contribute to our long-term values and goals. Separating these two may seem simple at first, but maintaining that can be challenging. The Eisenhower Matrix provides a clear framework for making decisions over and over and points out that consistency is the hard part, and it is what we need to focus on accomplishing.

Here are tools and techniques, described for your best use, to help you clarify the entire process behind the Eisenhower Box. As you study them, ask yourself two questions:

1. What am I working toward?
2. What are the core values that drive my life?

Answering these questions will help you clarify categories for certain tasks in your life. Deciding which tasks to do and which tasks to delete becomes much easier when you are clear about what is important to you.

Monkey management is a technique that involves identifying and prioritizing tasks that are critical to one's success and delegating or postponing the rest.[11]

This concept was coined by authors and time management experts Oncken Jr. & Wass.[12] It suggests that you should tackle your most important tasks first (the "monkeys") before moving on to less important tasks.[13] For example, if you have a crucial project due, work on that project before responding to emails or other less important tasks.

Eat the frog is a technique for tackling the most difficult or important task first thing in the morning to avoid procrastination

---

[11] William Oncken Jr., and Donald L. Wass, "Management Time: Who's Got the Monkey?" November-December 1999, accessed July 24, 2024, https://hbr.org/1999/11/management-time-whos-got-the-monkey.
[12] Ibid.
[13] Ibid.

and increase productivity.

This concept was popularized by Brian Tracy in his book *Eat That Frog!* It encourages you to tackle your most challenging or unpleasant task first thing in the morning so the rest of the day feels easier.[14] For example, if you dislike making cold calls, but it's a necessary part of your job, do it at the start of your workday.

Artwork by Sofia Duran-Stanton

The Pickle Jar Theory involves prioritizing tasks and filling up the proverbial pickle jar with the most important tasks first, followed by less important tasks, until the jar is full.

This is a metaphorical concept used in time management. Imagine your time as a pickle jar. Fill it with large, important tasks first (rocks); then fit smaller tasks around them (pebbles and sands),

---

[14]Brian Tracy, Eat That Frog!: 21 Great Ways to Stop Procrastinating and Get More Done in Less Time (San Francisco: Berrett-Koehler Publishers, 2007).

just like smaller objects fit around large ones in a jar. For example, schedule essential work tasks and family time first; then fit in hobbies and leisure activities around them.

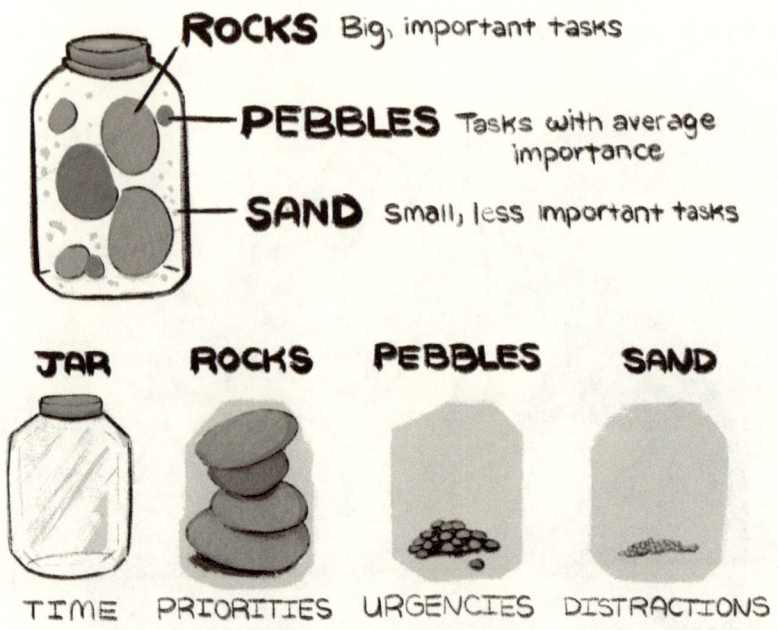

Artwork by Sofia Duran-Stanton

Time blocking is a technique that involves breaking up one's day into blocks of time and allocating specific tasks to each block. This ensures that you focus on one task at a time and not get distracted by other things.

This is a widely practiced time management technique without a specific originator. It involves breaking your day into blocks of time, each designated for specific tasks or activities. It helps you allocate time efficiently. For example, allocate a two-hour block for focused work, another for meetings, and a block for personal tasks, like exercise.

Artwork by Sofia Duran-Stanton

The Pomodoro Technique involves breaking up tasks into twenty-five-minute intervals, followed by short breaks to increase productivity and reduce burnout.[15]

This was developed by Francesco Cirillo in the late 1980s, inspired by a tomato-shaped kitchen timer.[16]

---

[15] Francesco Cirillo, The Pomodoro Technique: The Acclaimed Time-Management System That Has Transformed How We Work (New York: Currency, 2018).
[16] Ibid.

POMODORO TECHNIQUE

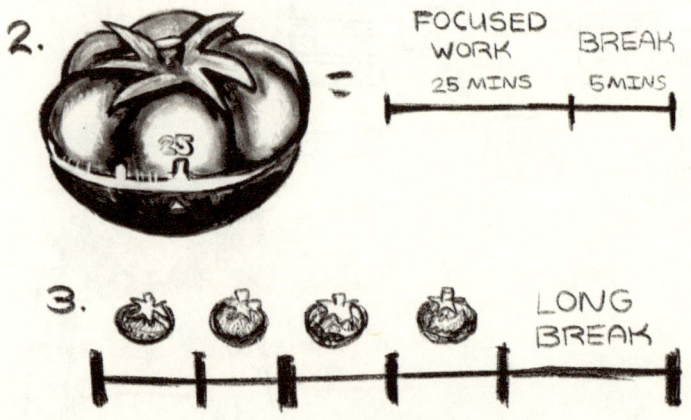

Artwork by Sofia Duran-Stanton

Parkinson's law is the idea that work expands to fill the time available for its completion, so setting artificial deadlines can increase productivity and reduce procrastination.[17]

This law is named after British historian and author Cyril Northcote Parkinson. It highlights the importance of setting deadlines. For example, setting a clear deadline for a report increases the likelihood of completing it efficiently.

Mind mapping involves visually organizing your ideas and tasks. It helps you see the big picture and prioritize tasks based on their importance.

This was popularized by Tony Buzan, a British author and educational consultant.[18] It's a visual representation of information,

---

[17] Cyril Northcote Parkinson, Parkinson's Law: And Other Studies in Administration (New York: Ballantine Books, 1968).
[18] Tony Buzan, "Mind Maps," 2017, accessed July 24, 2024, https://www.tonybuzan.edu.sg/about/mind-maps/.

used for brainstorming, organizing thoughts, and solving problems. Create a mind map to outline a project, connecting key ideas and subtasks.

The ABC Method involves categorizing tasks as A, B, or C based on their importance. Task A is the most important, followed by B and C tasks.

This is a fundamental concept in time management. Assign priorities (A for high priority, B for medium, C for low) to tasks, ensuring you focus on the most important ones first. A is an urgent report, B is nonurgent emails, and C is minor administrative tasks.

Time audit involves tracking how you spend your time for a week or two to identify areas to improve your time management.

This is a general time management practice with no single originator. It involves tracking how you spend your time to identify time-wasting activities and areas for improvement. Keep a detailed log of your daily activities for a week to see where your time goes.

Digital detox means taking a break from technology for a certain amount of time, which can help you be more present and productive.

The idea of a digital detox emerged with the widespread use of technology. It's about intentionally unplugging from digital devices to reduce distractions and reclaim time for more meaningful activities. Designate a specific period, like a weekend, to disconnect from screens and engage in off-line hobbies and social interactions.

Q&A with Kathy Lauren (from the intro)

Q: What are your thoughts about strategic future planning?

A: It's a self-care journey, trying to make time for myself. That's overwhelming, with student loans and New Year's resolutions.

Q: What is currently working well in your future planning?

A: Plan for life, school, taking a deep breath, schedule two to three weeks out, having self-love dates.

Q: What is currently *not* working well?

A: I often feel overwhelmed and doubt myself.

Q: What is your biggest challenge when it comes to future planning?

A: I'm afraid of making mistakes or not trying, and this affects my mental health.

Q: How do you feel about not having done the planning (future, time, career)?

A: I beat myself up, but I know everything happens for a reason, and you have to learn what's best for you. I get discouraged, but I must remind myself I'll get there.

Q: What have you tried already (future planning, time management, career progression)?

A: Planners, journals, talking to my boyfriend for positivity, and self-care.

Q: Why didn't it work? What was your investment?

A: I felt too overwhelmed.

Q: Why is it important to you to solve this challenge?

A: I set goals for myself, like having kids and improving myself to help my kids.

Q: What does your ideal situation look like?

A: I still have a plan to work on myself and create more goals. I want to continue to be happy.

Q: How will you know when you have achieved your goal?

A: I will be happy but still overwhelmed with new stuff.

Q: What would your life look like if this problem was gone?

A: Create more goals.

Q: When you achieve your goals, what will you be able to do?

A: Help people, give back through nursing, be there for people, and be kind.

CHAPTER 15

Wellness and the Zone of Genius

WELLNESS AND NEEDS

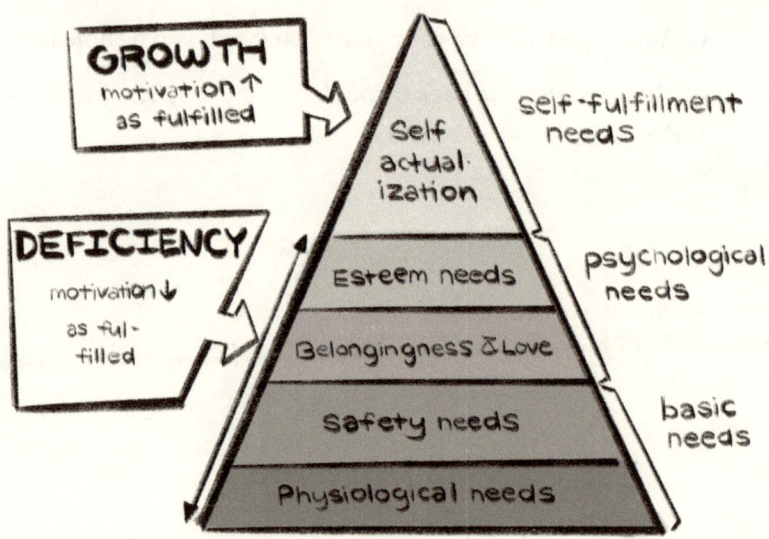

Artwork by Sofia Duran-Stanton

The concept of *ikigai*, finding one's sense of purpose, is closely linked to promoting overall wellness. Maslow's Hierarchy of Needs also emphasizes the importance of fulfilling one's needs to achieve self-actualization.[19]

---

[19] Saul McLeod, "Maslow's Hierarchy of Needs," January 24, 2024, accessed July 24, 2024, https://www.simplypsychology.org/maslow.html.

Maslow says that fulfilling basic and psychological needs is necessary but not sufficient for achieving motivation and personal growth. Only by fulfilling one's self-fulfillment needs, or growth needs, can one truly reach their full potential.[20]

According to Maslow's theory, fulfillment of the "lower deficiency needs" can curb one's motivation, while fulfillment of "growth needs" would further increase the motivation to excel. By aligning one's *ikigai* with their needs and goals, individuals can find greater fulfillment and overall wellness in their lives.[21]

THE ZONE OF GENIUS

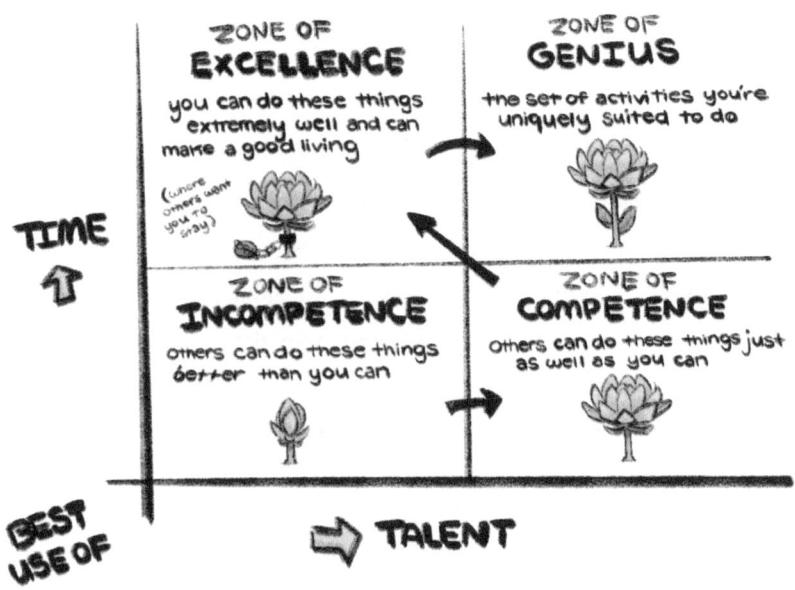

Artwork by Sofia Duran-Stanton

The concept of the Zone of Genius was introduced by Gay Hendricks in his book, *The Big Leap*.[22] The Zone of Genius is the area of your life

---

[20] Ibid.
[21] Ibid.
[22] Gay Hendricks, The Big Leap: Conquer Your Hidden Fear and Take Life to the Next Level (San Francisco: HarperOne, 2010).

where you are most passionate, talented, and fulfilled. This is where you can make your greatest contribution to the world.

The Zone of Excellence is the area where you are highly skilled and can work at a high level, but it may not be as fulfilling as the Zone of Genius.

The Zone of Competence is the area where you are competent at a certain task, but it does not bring you joy or fulfillment.[23]

The Zone of Incompetence is the area where you are not skilled or knowledgeable at all. It is important to identify each of these zones in your life and strive to spend more time in your Zone of Genius, as this is where you will find the most success and fulfillment. It's important for you to create a culture where employees are encouraged to find and work in their Zone of Genius, leading to higher job satisfaction and productivity.

WORK-LIFE BALANCE

General (retired) James C. McConville, the former chief of staff of the US Army, promoted the idea of "family first, always" as a critical component of achieving a healthy work-life balance.[24] He emphasized the importance of setting boundaries, being present, and prioritizing family time. He also acknowledged the challenges of balancing work and personal life but encourages individuals to strive for a balance that works for them and their loved ones.

---

[23]Hendricks, Gay. 2010. The Big Leap: Conquer Your Hidden Fear and Take Life to the Next Level. San Francisco: HarperOne.

[24] Haley Britzky, "The Army Chief of Staff Wants You to Have Work-Life Balance. Seriously," October 15, 2020, accessed July 24, 2024, https://taskandpurpose.com/news/army-chief-mcconville-people-priority/.

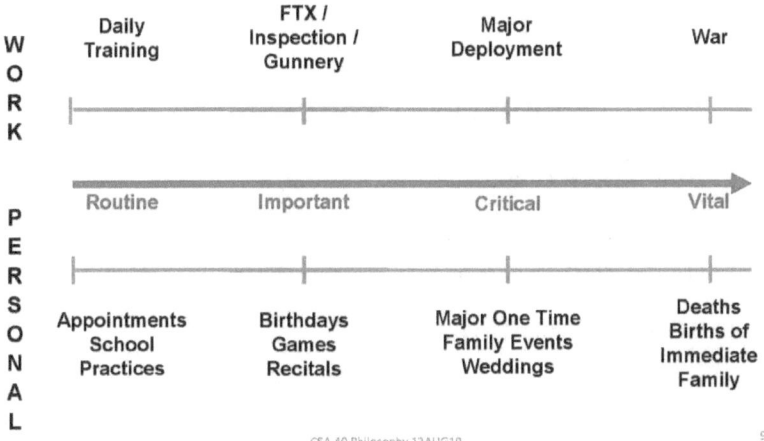

PART FOUR

Fundamentals Review and Workbook Preview

A PERSONAL ASSESSMENT

1. How **SMART** (**s**pecific, **m**easurable, **a**chievable, **r**elevant, and **t**ime-bound) are your goals?
2. How well do you manage your time?
3. What's your plan to do better?
4. Where do you see yourself in Maslow's Hierarchy of Needs?
5. What are your knowledge and skills for each zone (genius, excellence, competence, and incompetence)?

EXERCISES AND TAKEAWAYS

1. Pick three tools from the following list and map out how you will use them to improve your life: the Eisenhower Matrix, Monkey management, eat the frog, the Pickle Jar Theory, time blocking, the Pomodoro Technique, Parkinson's law, mind mapping, the ABC Method, time audit, and digital detox.
2. Identify where you are now in Maslow's Hierarchy of Needs and where you want to be. Identify your gaps and develop a plan to address the gaps. Align your *ikigai* with your needs and goals.
3. Review the zones and assess what your knowledge and skills are for each zone (genius, excellence, competence, and incompetence). Spend more time in your Zone of Genius.
4. What are your top three takeaways from each chapter (part four)?

CONCLUSION

Reflections of my Own Life Experiences

I was promoted to colonel in November 2023. I received many warm congratulations from fellow officers, friends, and family who came to support me. Some I served with date back to when I was a seventeen-year-old private.

Later that night, after my family was asleep, I had some time to reflect when I was alone in the kitchen.

I thought about the sacrifices of my Filipino grandfather, Second Lieutenant Melecio Duran, who valiantly served side by side with American soldiers in World War II, specifically during the infamous Bataan Death March, where he and others died for our freedom. I thought of the enduring legacy he and others have imparted and the vital role that representation plays in the modern Army and in my personal life.

I realized how privileged I am to be living proof of the ideals and values my grandfather fought for. His resilience and sacrifice serve as the bedrock upon which I have built my career. To me, *building the bench* is a concept deeply intertwined with our history. It means ensuring that future generations of Filipina Americans and women like me find opportunities to not just join our ranks but to thrive in whatever type of service we choose.

I was reminded of why I chose a life of service in the first place and why it's so important to me to continue in new and challenging ways. That's just the point. While I have accomplished a lot so far in my life, there is more to do. My commitment and passion to service continues, and I pay attention to my own words. In this book, I should be suitably inspired to find new challenges that are worthwhile for me and for the people I can serve. I hope you will be inspired to do the same.

As a Filipina American, I come from humble beginnings and was able to take advantage of all the opportunities I was offered. I certainly could not do it all alone, without the support of my family, friends, colleagues, mentors, and sponsors along the way.

Without the foundation of the women who shaped me in my formative years, I would not be where I am today. I am a product of my strong upbringing, and I am thankful every day for the experience I had growing up. The paths I have taken and the emotional roller coaster I felt while writing this have provided me insights into how fortunate I am and how proud I am to be Filipina.

This fortune comes from having experienced life as a Filipina with a rich culture, community, and the importance of family. Now, as I mentor other young leaders and subordinates, I emphasize the importance of appreciating where they came from and embracing it. I know and appreciate the value of mentorship and guidance. It is important to share our stories with others. Sharing not only helps them but is also critical for understanding ourselves.

After my special promotion day, as I was reflecting on my life that night, I was thinking of how the event helped me realize that all the concepts I have shared in this book have come full circle as I experience my own LOTUS within.

And like all other women who have full-time jobs, regardless of whether they are the CEO of a large organization earning a living, I can imagine that when they come home, they are still the ones who assume the role of washing the dishes, cleaning the table, sweeping the floor, scrubbing the toilet bowls, and tending to their family's needs as wives and mothers.

We often neglect ourselves to our detriment, so I hope this book and its exercises will allow you to take a knee and focus on yourself so that you can continue to be a beacon of light in your passion to inherently serve others.

Next, in part five, you will find a workbook version of what I've presented here in the book, which is an opportunity to explore and do your best to answer the questions. Only when you stand up to the challenges offered here will you be able to make substantial and meaningful changes in your life and the lives of your loved ones.

Good luck!

PART FIVE

THE WORKBOOK

LOTUS

LIFE OF TIMELESS UNBOUND STRATEGIES

Grow your purpose and ignite your passion.

A PERSONAL ASSESSMENT

Before you continue, I highly recommend you start writing on a journal and take some time to answer these questions as best as you can. I'm sure you'll soon discover more about yourself, which will change at least some of your answers. In fact, you'll have a chance to *re*assess yourself at the end of part one.

1. Describe the importance of future planning and how you currently plan for your future.
2. What is your biggest challenge when it comes to planning your future?
3. Describe how you currently prioritize.
4. What is your biggest challenge in prioritizing?
5. Describe how you currently manage your time.
6. What is your biggest challenge in time management?
7. Describe the process of how you make important decisions that affect your future.
8. What is your biggest challenge in decision-making for future outcomes?

PART ONE

What Is Your Why?

In today's fast-paced world, many women juggle multiple roles, defining their professional careers and personal lives. With so much on their plates, it's no surprise that they can become overwhelmed and lose sight of their goals and passions. That's why it's especially crucial for professional women to take the time to strategically plan their lives, find their passion, prioritize, and manage their time effectively. Strategic life planning will allow you to identify your passions and align your personal and professional goals accordingly. By prioritizing your tasks and responsibilities, you can ensure that you are making the most of your time and energy.

Effective time management is also critical. By creating a schedule and sticking to it, you can maximize your productivity while still leaving time for self-care and important activities. This means saying "No" to unnecessary obligations and delegating tasks to others when possible.

Strategic life planning is not a one-time event. It's an ongoing process. This process requires dedication, commitment, and a willingness to adjust as needed. With the right mindset and approach, you can successfully navigate your many roles, keep multiple balls in the air, and achieve success in all aspects of your life.

CHAPTER 1

Mistakes and Secrets

Here are ten common mistakes professional women make when strategically planning their lives, especially when they do not prioritize themselves or manage their time effectively:

1. Not taking the time to reflect on values and passions before making life decisions.
2. Failing to prioritize self-care and neglecting physical, mental, and emotional health.
3. Overcommitting and taking on too many responsibilities.
4. Not setting clear goals and objectives for personal and professional purposes.
5. Being too rigid in their plans and failing to adapt to changing circumstances.
6. Not delegating tasks effectively or failing to ask for help when needed.
7. Failing to recognize the importance of downtime and relaxation in preventing burnout.
8. Getting caught up in minor tasks and losing sight of the bigger picture.
9. Procrastinating or putting off important tasks until the last minute.

10. Being unrealistic about the time and energy needed for tasks and responsibilities.

Here are ten secrets that professional women can use to strategically plan their lives, prioritize themselves, and manage their time effectively:

1. Take time to reflect on values, passions, and long-term goals before making decisions.
2. Prioritize self-care and reduce stress with exercise, healthy food, meditation, and yoga.
3. Use a planner or calendar to schedule time for work and personal responsibilities.
4. Set realistic goals and break them down into smaller, manageable tasks.
5. Learn to say "No" to commitments that do not align with your goals or values.
6. Delegate tasks effectively and ask for help when needed.
7. Make time for downtime and relaxation to prevent burnout and recharge your batteries.
8. Focus on high-value tasks and avoid getting bogged down by low-priority distractions.
9. Set boundaries around your time and learn to prioritize your own needs.
10. Reassess and adjust plans as circumstances change or you achieve your goals.

By following these secrets, professional women can create a more balanced and fulfilling life while still achieving their personal and professional goals.

CHAPTER 2

The Importance of Self-Care in Strategic Life Planning

Write down how you currently take care of yourself per each topic below and how you can further improve. Write SMART (specific, measurable, attainable, relevant, time-bound) goals for each.

—Holistic health.

—Physical self-care.

—Mental self-care.

—Spiritual self-care.

—Psychological self-care.

—Self-care is not selfish.

—Strategic self-care.

—It is about you!

CHAPTER 3

Finding Your Ikigai

Ikigai is a Japanese concept that roughly translates to "a reason for being." It is a combination of passion, mission, vocation, and profession that gives your life purpose and meaning. According to the Japanese, everyone has an *ikigai*, but it takes time and effort to discover it. In this chapter, we will explore the concept of *ikigai* and how you can find your own.

To find your *ikigai*, you first need to understand what it means. As mentioned earlier, *ikigai* is a combination of passion, mission, vocation, and profession.

Step 1: Identify your passions.

Step 2: Determine your mission.

Step 3: Recognize your talents.

Step 4: Find your profession.

Step 5: Combine your passions, mission, talents, and profession.

LIVING YOUR *IKIGAI*

Set goals.

Act.

Embrace challenges.

Surround yourself with supportive people.

Be patient.

CHAPTER 4

Writing Your Obituary

Why write your obituary?

Control your legacy.

Reduce the burden on your loved ones.

Reflect on your life.

Step 1: Gather information.

Step 2: Decide on the tone.

Step 3: Write a draft.

Step 4: Revise and edit.

Step 5: Share your wishes.

CHAPTER 5

Discovering Your "Why"

When it comes to strategic life planning, identifying your passion, prioritization, and time management, it is easy to get caught up in the *what* and *how* of achieving your goals. However, it is equally important to explore the *why*—the underlying motivation and purpose that drives your actions.

But how do you discover your *why* and define your *ikigai*? Here are steps you can take:

Reflect on your past experiences.

Identify your core values.

Visualize your ideal future.

Experiment and explore.

HOW TO REFLECT ON YOUR CHILDHOOD

Step 1: Create a safe space.

Step 2: Gather memories.

Step 3: Journal.

Step 4: Seek support.

WHAT TO LOOK FOR WHEN REFLECTING ON YOUR CHILDHOOD

Relationships with caregivers.

Family dynamics.

Traumatic experiences.

Interests and passions.

As you reflect on each phase, ask yourself questions:

What were the defining moments or experiences during this time?

Who were the people that influenced me the most?

What were the challenges I faced?

What were the successes I achieved?

What were the lessons I learned?

What was the significance of this milestone for me at the time?

What did I learn from achieving this milestone?

How did this milestone impact my life going forward?

Did achieving this milestone align with my values and passions?

Was this milestone part of my larger goal or plan for myself?

A PERSONAL ASSESSMENT

1. Describe the importance of future planning and how you currently plan for your future.
2. What is your biggest challenge when it comes to planning your future?
3. Describe how you currently prioritize.
4. What is your biggest challenge in prioritizing?

5. Describe how you currently manage your time.
6. What is your biggest challenge in time management?
7. Describe the process of how you make important decisions that affect your future.
8. What is your biggest challenge in decision-making for future outcomes?

EXERCISES AND TAKEAWAYS

1. Write your obituary.
2. Explore your *why* (passion, values, strengths, fears).
3. Reflect on your past self.
4. Analyze your current strategies for planning your life.
5. Evaluate how you prioritize and manage your time.
6. Write down your top three takeaways from each chapter (part one).
7. Write down any questions and discuss them with your mentor, sponsor, or coach.

PART TWO

What Is Your Strategy for the Future?

There will be no one else like you—ever!

This simple fact should prompt each of us to ask ourselves a few basic questions.

What wakes you up in the morning?

Why do you think you are here?

What were you born to do?

What does success mean in our culture and society?

What does having purpose really mean, and how does it vary from person to person?

How do we measure improvement?

How can we measure our adaptive skills?

CHAPTER 6

The Arc of Improvement

Write down how you can improve on each of the topics below. Write SMART (specific, measurable, attainable, relevant, time-bound) goals for each.

—Conscious effort

—The meaning of success

—Fulfillment

—Growth

—Financial stability

—Occupational awareness

—Continuous process improvement

CHAPTER 7

Evaluate Your Current State of Self

Knowing your current self is essential for planning your future. By understanding who you are right now and what you want to achieve, you can create a strategic plan that aligns with your values, passions, and goals. Regular self-assessment and feedback from others can help you stay on track and adjust as needed, ensuring that you continue to grow and thrive.

CHAPTER 8

Reverse Engineer Your Plan

Create a timeline.

> "How did I get here?"
>
> "Did I plan well enough?"
>
> "How can I fix my mistakes and lack of planning?"
>
> What will be your legacy?
>
> What are the things you want your children and grandchildren to remember?

BIG ROCKS AND LITTLE ROCKS

Big Rocks symbolize our priorities. They encompass the tasks, projects, or goals each of us must accomplish. They define our mission-critical objectives and do *not* include items on anyone's messy to-do list.

> *What are your big rocks?*
>
> *What is your next set of big rocks?*
>
> *What is your next set of big and medium rocks?*
>
> *What is your next set of big, medium, and little rocks?*

A PERSONAL ASSESSMENT

1. What does "success" mean to you?
2. How are you strategizing your purpose in life, a.k.a. your *why*?
3. What *is* your *why*?
4. What makes you unique?
5. How do you measure improvement?
6. How do you measure your adaptive skills?
7. What conscious efforts do you make in planning your daily activities?
8. Are you living a life that is aligned with your values, passions, and purpose?
9. Do you have financial stability, and if not, what is your plan to achieve it?
10. How would you rate your occupational awareness?

EXERCISES AND TAKEAWAYS

1. What are your big rocks in life?
2. What are your thirty-year big rocks?
3. What are your twenty-year big rocks?
4. What are your ten-year big rocks?
5. What are your five-year big rocks?
6. What are your annual big rocks?
7. What are your daily big rocks?
8. What are your top three takeaways from each chapter (part two)?

PART THREE

How Do You Prioritize?

Prioritization is the key to effective strategic life planning. Without it, you may find yourself overwhelmed with too many tasks and not enough time to accomplish them all. Prioritization helps you focus on the most important things in your life and ensures that you're using your time and resources effectively.

CHAPTER 9

Why? How? What?

The Golden Circle consists of three concentric circles: the "Why" in the center, surrounded by the "How," and finally, the "What." The Golden Circle emphasizes the importance of purpose-driven leadership and encourages organizations to focus on their beliefs and values to drive success.

Draw your own Golden Circle and answer the following:

What is your *why*?

What is your purpose?

How do you get after your w*hy*?

What do you do now?

What should you be doing?

CHAPTER 10

Conducting a SWOT Analysis

SWOT stands for strengths, weaknesses, opportunities, and threats. A professional SWOT analysis is valuable. I have used them to help individuals on a personal and professional level and to help organizations based on collective SWOT analyses from different people inside their team.

Complete two SWOT analyses: personal and professional. Compare and contrast the two. How can you continue to improve reviewing these SWOT analyses?

CHAPTER 11

The 7 Habits of Highly Effective People

Incorporate each of the seven habits in your life. What can you do now for each of these habits?

Habit 1: Be proactive.

Habit 2: Begin with the end in mind and create a career timeline that takes into consideration the following.

Habit 3: Put first things first and think of big rocks and little rocks.

Habit 4: Think win-win.

Habit 5: Seek first to understand, then to be understood.

Habit 6: Synergize.

Habit 7: Sharpen the saw.

CHAPTER 12

Prioritization Tools

Try each of these tools, and write them down. Similar to "The Golden Circle," *why* would you use one over the other, *how* would you use each one, and in what circumstances would you use each one? Find out what other prioritization tools could work for you.

The Worth-Your-Time Test.

The RAG Rating System.

The GTD Method.

Pareto analysis.

Failing to plan is planning to fail.

A PERSONAL ASSESSMENT

1. What are your big rocks (BR) and little rocks (LR)?
2. What is your *why*?
3. What is your purpose?
4. How do you get after your *why*?
5. What do you do now?
6. What should you be doing?
7. What are your most effective habits?
8. What are your most ineffective habits?
9. Where would you rate yourself when it comes to prioritizing?
10. How could you improve?

EXERCISES AND TAKEAWAYS

1. Draw your own Golden Circle.
2. Do your own SWOT analysis (strengths, weaknesses, opportunities, and threats).
3. If you could ask yourself one honest question, what would it be?
4. Incorporate each of the seven habits in your life.
5. Try each of the prioritization tools and see which ones work best for you.
6. What are your top three takeaways from each chapter (part three)?

PART FOUR

Can You Manage Your Time?

Managing free time effectively is important for personal well-being and productivity. Here are some general strategies:

1. *Set clear goals.*
2. *Prioritize self-care.*
3. *Time block.*
4. *Limit distractions.*
5. *Learn something new.*
6. *Spend quality time with loved ones.*
7. *Volunteer and give back.*
8. *Plan ahead.*
9. *Delegate and outsource.*
10. *Be flexible and adaptable.*

DO!

1. Set clear goals—define your short-term and long-term goals to stay focused.
2. Prioritize tasks—identify high-priority tasks and tackle them first.
3. Use time blocks—allocate specific time blocks for different activities.
4. Delegate when possible—don't be afraid to delegate tasks to others.
5. Take short breaks—schedule short breaks to recharge and stay productive.
6. Learn to say no—politely decline tasks that don't align with your goals.
7. Use technology wisely—utilize productivity apps and tools to streamline tasks.
8. Create a routine (battle rhythm)—plan on daily, weekly, and monthly schedules to stay organized.
9. Batch similar tasks—group similar activities to minimize context-switching.
10. Reflect and adjust—regularly assess your time management strategies and make necessary adjustments.

DON'T!

1. Procrastinate—avoid putting off important tasks for later.
2. Overcommit—be mindful not to take on too many responsibilities.
3. Multitask unnecessarily—focus on one task at a time to increase efficiency.
4. Ignore self-care—neglecting self-care can lead to burnout; make time for it.
5. Micromanage—trust others to handle tasks without constant supervision.
6. Let distractions rule—minimize interruptions and distractions.
7. Fail to set boundaries—establish boundaries to protect your time.
8. Waste time on low-value activities—be selective about how you spend your time.
9. Rush through tasks—quality is often more important than speed.
10. Neglect personal growth—allocate time for learning and self-improvement.

CHAPTER 13

How to Write SMART Goals

SMART stands for specific, measurable, achievable, relevant, and time-bound. Use these examples to create your own.

SMART Goal #1: Career advancement.

SMART Goal #2: Improve time management skills in six months.

SMART Goal #3: Improve prioritization skills in one month.

SMART Goal #4: Improve your two-mile run time from nineteen minutes to fifteen minutes in four months.

CHAPTER 14

Tools to Help You Manage Time

These are the tools we covered to help you manage your time: The Eisenhower Matrix, Monkey management, eat the frog, the Pickle Jar Theory, time blocking, the Pomodoro Technique, Parkinson's law, mind mapping, the ABC Method, time audit, and digital detox.

CHAPTER 15

Wellness and the Zone of Genius

The concept of *ikigai*, or finding one's sense of purpose, is closely linked to promoting overall wellness. Maslow's hierarchy of needs also emphasizes the importance of fulfilling one's needs to achieve self-actualization.

The concept of the Zone of Genius was introduced by Gay Hendricks in *The Big Leap*. The Zone of Genius is the area of your life where you are most passionate, talented, and fulfilled. This is where you can make your greatest contribution to the world.

The Zone of Excellence is the area where you are highly skilled and can work at a high level, but it may not be as fulfilling as the Zone of Genius.

The Zone of Competence is the area where you are competent at a certain task, but it does not bring you joy or fulfillment.

The Zone of Incompetence is the area where you are not skilled or knowledgeable at all.

A PERSONAL ASSESSMENT

1. How SMART (specific, measurable, achievable, relevant, and time-bound) are your goals?
2. How well do you manage your time?
3. What's your plan to do better?
4. Where do you see yourself in Maslow's Hierarchy of Needs?

5. What are your knowledge and skills for each zone (genius, excellence, competence, and incompetence)?

EXERCISES AND TAKEAWAYS

Make an effort to try at least two of the time management tools a week until you've had the chance to try them all. Select what will work best for you based on what you need to accomplish and your preference.

1. Write down when you found each one useful and why.
2. What other time management tool(s) do you use or learn about that are not listed?
3. Identify where you are now in Maslow's Hierarchy of Needs and where you want to be. Identify your gaps and develop a plan to address the gaps. Align your *ikigai* with your needs and goals.
4. Review the zones and assess what your knowledge and skills are for each zone (genius, excellence, competence, and incompetence). Spend more time in your Zone of Genius.
5. What are your top three takeaways from each chapter (part four)?

ACKNOWLEDGMENTS

Standing on the Shoulders of Giants

We stand on the shoulders of giants, those who came before us, broke barriers, and paved the way for our journey. My grandfather and countless others like him were giants. Their stories resonate with me as a Filipina American, but they should resonate with all of us as examples of unwavering dedication to duty and service.

When it comes to this book, I have several people to thank. The cloth of my career is interwoven with many experiences. Networking has been a key aspect of my career. I would like to thank those I have met along my career path who have contributed to the success I have enjoyed in my life. Building connections, sharing knowledge, and fostering teamwork are essential. By collaborating with diverse groups of individuals, we not only learn and grow but also represent our backgrounds and perspectives. Thanks to all of you who have been part of this journey with me.

"Dacal pung salamat karetang kamaganak ku keng Pilipinas at maraming salamat po sa mga pamilya ko sa buhong mundo."

To David Tabatsky and Nancy Rosenfeld for their help and confidence in getting me through the publication process. To John Koehler and Joe Coccaro for believing in the value of what the book offers, and to the Koehler Books staff for helping me get to the finish line. Thank you to all the leaders, friends, and colleagues who provided their time and energy in helping me refine this project as well as those who provided their endorsement of support for a valuable initiative in helping women.

On a deeply personal note, I want to extend my gratitude to my husband and my children. They have been my unwavering support system, enabling me to pursue my career. Their love, understanding, and sacrifice have allowed me to dedicate myself to this noble profession. It is often said that behind every great leader is a strong support system, and I stand here today, a testament to the truth of that statement.

Let us remember that representation matters. It matters to every individual who looks at us and sees the possibility of achieving their dreams. Diversity and inclusivity are the building blocks of our strength and resilience. Let us continue to honor the legacy of those who came before us by building a brighter future for all. Together, we shall reach new heights, forge new horizons, and uphold the values that make us great.

And last, thank you to those who are discovering their "LOTUS within" by joining me on this journey.

REFERENCES

Britzky, Haley. 2020. "The Army Chief of Staff Wants You to Have Work-Life Balance. Seriously." October 15. Accessed July 24, 2024. https://taskandpurpose.com/news/army-chief-mcconville-people-priority/.

Buzan, Tony. 2017. "Mind Maps." Accessed July 24, 2024. https://www.tonybuzan.edu.sg/about/mind-maps/.

Cirillo, Francesco. 2018. *The Pomodoro Technique: The Acclaimed Time-Management System That Has Transformed How We Work.* New York: Currency.

Clear, James. 2024. "How to Be More Productive and Eliminate Time Wasting Activities by Using the 'Eisenhower Box.'" Accessed July 24, 2024. https://jamesclear.com/eisenhower-box.

Covey, Stephen. 1989. *The 7 Habits of Highly Effective People.* New York: Simon and Schuster.

Hendricks, Gay. 2010. *The Big Leap: Conquer Your Hidden Fear and Take Life to the Next Level.* San Francisco: HarperOne.

McLeod, Saul. 2024. "Maslow's Hierarchy of Needs." January 24. Accessed July 24, 2024. https://www.simplypsychology.org/maslow.html.

Oncken, William Jr., and Donald L. Wass. 1999. "Management Time: Who's Got the Monkey?" November-December. Accessed July 24, 2024. https://hbr.org/1999/11/management-time-whos-got-the-monkey.

Parkinson, Cyril Northcote. 1968. *Parkinson's Law: And Other Studies in Administration.* New York: Ballantine Books.

Sinek, Simon. 2024. "Simon Sinek." July 24. Accessed July 24, 2024. https://simonsinek.com/golden-circle/.

Tracy, Brian. 2007. *Eat That Frog!: 21 Great Ways to Stop Procrastinating and Get More Done in Less Time.* San Francisco: Berrett-Koehler Publishers.

www.ingramcontent.com/pod-product-compliance
Lightning Source LLC
LaVergne TN
LVHW041948070526
838199LV00051BA/2944